TURNING AROUND

TURNING

THE UPSIDE-

AROUND

DOWN KIDS

HELPING DYSLEXIC
KIDS OVERCOME
THEIR DISORDER

HAROLD N. LEVINSON, M.D.
AND ADDIE SANDERS

M. EVANS & COMPANY, INC.   NEW YORK

M. Evans and Company, Inc.
216 East 49th Street
New York, New York 10017

Manufactured in the United States of America

9 8 7 6 5 4 3 2 1

Illustrations by Daniel J. Hochstatter
Typesetting by AeroType, Inc.

Library of Congress Cataloging-in-Publication Data

Levinson, Harold N.

Turning around the upside-down kids: helping dyslexic
kids overcome their disorder / Harold Levinson and
Addie Meyer Sanders.
  p.   cm
Another work in the authors' "upside-down kids"
trilogy.
  Includes bibliographic references (p.).
  ISBN 0-87131-700-1 : $17.95
  1. Dyslexic children—Education—Case studies.
2. Dyslexia—Case studies. 3. Interpersonal relations.
I. Sanders, Addie. II. Title.
LC4708.L48 1992
371.91'44—dc20   92-13440
                                                CIP

Contents

Dedication

To Sue Stafford—and all other teachers and professionals dedicated to helping dyslexics. Because of Sue's dyslexia and its successful outcome, as well as her gifted intuition and teaching abilities, she was especially empowered with the empathy, skill and determination needed to help thousands and thousands of dyslexics and their families.

Having worked with Sue for years, I felt the need to clone her as Ms. Jensen in *The Upside-Down Kids*. Hopefully, she will thus be able to help thousands and thousands of others.

Introduction
For Adults

THE PRIMARY AIM of the trilogy entitled *The Upside-Down Kids* is clear—to provide the reader and listener with a *simple* but comprehensive understanding of *all* the symptoms and helpful therapies characterizing dyslexia and dyslexics. This book and trilogy of *diagnostic and therapeutic novels* represents my best attempt at resolving the complex series of goals underlying the following questions:

• How do you best provide millions and millions of kids, as well as their loving parents and involved professionals, with everything vital there is to know about their defining symptoms and helpful therapies in dyslexia?

- How can you do it in as simple and clear a manner as possible?
- How do you maximize empathy, interest, and concentration, regardless of age?
- How might this content have the impact of reality—an impact sufficient to overcome the denials and hopelessness of those with dyslexia?
- How can this impact be used therapeutically so as to reverse emotional scarring and feelings of stupidity, ugliness, craziness...?
- How do you write a book for children which is also fully capable of providing the insight and language needed by adults to regain and maintain *therapeutic contact* with emotionally traumatized and thus defensive kids?
- How can interested professions be *shown* all the educational, psychological and medical methods needed to help dyslexics *turn around*?
- And finally, how can Upside-Down Kids be made to function and feel *right-side up*?

By using a simplistic style and an evolving dialogue between eight dyslexic kids and a dedicated teacher, "life-saving" information is conveyed in a natural and easy to digest fashion. This style is especially good to enhance the reader's interest, concentration, and even memory, while providing all the vital insights needed to reverse the emotional, academic, and physiological symptoms typifying this devastating and heretofore puzzling disorder.

Having medically and psychologically tested over 25,000 dyslexics, I know full well that providing upside-down kids with real, down-to-earth, tangible insight is absolutely essential for catalyzing the healing process—for reversing their feeling dumb, ugly, lazy, stupid, inept, klutzy, crazy...

Since insight alone is insufficient to compensate for either the inner physiological core of the dyslexic disorder or its symptomatic fall-out (affecting reading, writing, spelling, math, memory, speech, sense of direction and time, concentration and activity levels, balance and coordination), upside-down kids must receive additional help. As a result, *Turning Around: The Upside-Down Kids* specifically illustrates and explains how each of many and varied dyslexia therapies work, including the use of a new, revolutionary treatment which rapidly and efficiently helps 75% of treated cases.

Additionally, the content within this book and trilogy attempts to teach dyslexics and/or their interested parents and professionals:

- that all symptoms are like coded messages which must be deciphered rather than denied or criticized away; i.e., dyslexics invariably lose their place when they read and need to slow down their reading speed and use a finger so as to compensate for an underlying impairment in eye-tracking capacity.
- that everything said and done, especially in a therapeutic setting, must be carefully analyzed; i.e., to dramatize these points dreams were interpreted as was name-calling. Eight kids were deliberately chosen to symbolically reflect the eight letters in dyslexia, and even the easy-to-read typeface is used to enhance the eye tracking capacity of dyslexics with defective "missile eyes."
- that dyslexics are most helped when holistically treated via multiple therapies and therapists; i.e., that's why both a teacher and Dr. L. were chosen to educate and treat the children in a manner

which could be duplicated by other combined educational/clinical teams.

• that any valid conception of dyslexia must be fully capable of encompassing and explaining *all* known symptoms and helpful therapies; otherwise, something is wrong.

It is anticipated that the dissemination and use of the content of this book and trilogy will save millions of dyslexic kids from lives doomed by endless frustration, failure and impaired self-esteem.

Introduction
For Kids

BEFORE THIS STORY BEGINS, let me introduce you once again to the 8 Upside-Down Kids. The 8 kids are very special. They hold the important clues needed to solve a very complicated puzzle. And the name of this puzzle has 8 letters—*dyslexia*.

A very interested and smart teacher has already helped them find out why they are not like other normal or Right-Side-Up Kids; why smart kids sometimes feel dumb. And with Dr. L's help, she's even going to straighten them out. That's what this story is all about: how to help dyslexic kids get better. That's why this story is called *Turning Around: The Upside-Down Kids*.

Listen very carefully to *all* the different ways

there are of helping these Upside-Down Kids; and why these treatment methods work.

Listen very carefully to how all their many and frustrating symptoms disappear—almost by magic. If we can really, really understand these kids and the methods needed to help *straighten* them out, we can also help millions and millions of other Upside-Down Kids. And as we said in the last story, we can even prevent these kids from growing up to be Upside-Down Adults.

Now here are the 8 Upside-Down Kids:

1. Kram—the football ram, a great athlete who can't even read his name without seeing the letters jumping all over the page.
2. Anna—the know-it-all "motor-mouth" who can't even write her name.
3. Funny-Freddie—the clown who can't even spell his name.
4. Hyper-Harry—the hyperactive klutz who has difficulty with directions like right and left and telling time, and even simple addition and subtraction without using fingers and toes.
5. Bob-the-Fog—who can't concentrate or even hear

words clearly—he always wears a baseball cap for some unknown reason.

6. Randy-the-Magician—who magically seems to forget whatever he sees, hears, or does—especially math problems.

7. Silent Amy—who can't even speak her name without stumbling, mumbling, or stuttering.

8. Chuck—the mean, lean rebel, a defiant terror.

Each of the eight Upside-Down Kids is unique and very special. Yet they all have many things in common. They have important things to say. Listen to them very carefully. Let's get to know them all really well. They're all very worthwhile understanding and helping.

1

Morning Scare

6:15 A.M.

The middle school's running track was almost empty. Only one person ran. Her feet pounded the blacktop. Tap, tap, tap. Her heart fell into the rhythm. Thump, thump, thump. Her arms swung back and forth. Pump, pump, pump. Her breathing became regular. Her body raced as if set on automatic pilot. And finally her mind felt free, clear and focused, fine tuned by the running motion.

There was a coolness in the air. A gray dawn filled the eastern sky. But ribbons of bright pink fought their way into it. Dark clouds circled above her head, whipping the wind past her face. A promise of colder days ahead. Mary Jensen suddenly realized, for the first time, that she was totally alone on the track. In September, there had been at least a half dozen runners. By the end of October, the number was down to two or three. But today, she was alone.

A chill suddenly slid down her spine. She shivered. Beads of sweat broke out on her forehead. She quickly looked from side to side. There it was again. That awful feeling. That feeling that she was being watched.

She'd felt that way for almost two weeks now. Tap, tap, tap. She tried to keep her feet running at a steady pace, even though her heart began racing out of control. Fear. She neared the end of the track. The end farthest away from the school. The end closest to the thick dark woods creeping with long black shadows. Empty branches reached out to her like long skinny arms. Gasping for breath she pushed on. Tap, tap, tap. Her feet moved her closer and closer to the dark woods.

Suddenly a movement. A man. No, a boy. A large boy stepped out from the shadows. His dark eyes were filled with the mystery of the forest. His eyes caught hers. Held them.

Gasping, Mary Jensen stopped. Only her feet moved, running in place now. It was Chuck. Defiant

Chuck from her class. Chuck-the-Terror. Feared by everyone in school. He'd given others more bloody noses and black eyes than anyone else. Chuck who sat in the back of her classroom since school began—his arms folded tightly across his chest. Hands hidden deep in his armpits. Defiant. Grumbling or growling. Never doing any work. Never really part of the class. Ms. Jensen wondered if she would ever reach him. And now, here he was facing her. Alone. What did he want?

She tried calming her racing heart while her feet ran in place. Tap, tap, tap. She searched Chuck's face to see what he wanted. A cool wind from the north wiped the sweat from her face. Why didn't he say something? she wondered.

Soon she started to breathe easier. Somehow she knew he wasn't there to harm her. Suddenly she realized he was the one who had been watching her all these mornings. He had waited until she was alone. Until he got up enough nerve. Then he showed himself. Tap, tap, tap continued her racing heart.

Ms. Jensen looked at the track. Then back to Chuck. She cocked her head and eyes towards the track. An invitation to run with her. Then she started moving ahead. Past the woods. Tap, tap, tap.

She moved slowly at first, listening for Chuck to follow. Soon she heard his steps behind her. Moving closer. Clump, clump, clump. He was just behind her. When next to her, she speeded up to her regular pace. And he let his pace match hers. Tap, tap, clump, clump. For the very first time, they ran together. Were together. Chuck had finally made contact. A miracle. Will it last?

Pinkish-purple dawn lightened the sky. Golden strands of angel hair broke through the early haze lighting the track. It looked like they were running through a spun-gold tunnel.

Ms. Jensen was delighted. Chuck was running with her, not away from her. All too often, she didn't think she was getting through to him at all. In fact, she sometimes thought he really hated her. Especially after her visit in his home. Tap, tap, clump, clump. They passed the school building together. All the rooms stood dark and still.

Ms. Jensen's mind wandered back to the day she had visited Chuck's parents. At their home.

They had no phone so she couldn't call. She had sent notes home with Chuck, saying she wanted to meet with them. But there was never an answer. She doubted if Chuck ever gave his parents the notes. So she went to his home. Alone. Unannounced. Uninvited.

The house was old and small. A tar paper shack down by the river. Brown cardboard covered shattered glass windows. Old papers and cans filled the yard. She knocked gently. But even so, the door swung open to her touch as if she pushed it. The lock was broken—just like everything else.

Her eyes gazed around the shack. It had only one tiny room. In the center, on a tumbled bed propped up by many old pillows, sat a sick, bony, gray-haired woman. Chuck stood next to the bed. He looked up, shocked to see his teacher. He glared at Ms. Jensen. She knew if looks could kill...she would be dead.

"Who's dat? Whad'ya want?" screeched the old and tired-looking woman.

"Ma. It's okay. Dat's my teach," Chuck grumbled through clenched teeth.

"Yes, Mrs. Storm. I'm Chuck's teacher and I..." But Ms. Jensen never finished her sentence.

CRASH! The door slammed open. The whole house shook. A voice, like thunder, filled the room. "Who da hell are you?"

The old woman bent over, coughing. Chuck grabbed a basin and gave it to her.

"I'm Chuck's teach..." Ms. Jensen started to explain. But the big man's fist slammed down on the table interrupting her. Dirty dishes flew to the floor.

His booming breath, heavy with liquor, filled the room. Fire lit up the big man's eyes. He raised his fist, shaking it at Chuck. "Whatsa matta? He been bad? Give ya trouble? I'll take care of my own." His fist crashed onto the table again. "He ain't no good. I'll fix 'im for ya." A mean grin filled the old man's face. He started towards his son, shaking his huge fist in the air. But his foot caught on the table leg. And he fell, crashing to the floor in a giant heap. Grumbling and cursing, he pulled himself back up.

Ms. Jensen moved so that her small frame stood between father and son. Calmly she said, "No. No problem."

"No problem?" the big man shouted. "Then get

out, lady. You have a problem with my boy, I'll handle it. No problem, then you leave us alone. Boy, where's my supper? What d'ya have to do to get some grub 'round here?"

Ms. Jensen looked at Chuck; his eyes told her nothing. They resembled dark pools of hate. Now she fully understood why he acted the way he did.

Tap, tap, clump, clump. Her mind returned to the track. To Chuck running beside her. After that visit, Ms. Jensen understood Chuck better. Now she knew why he couldn't play football on the team: he had to go home and care for his sick mother. Why he hid his feelings and acted mean—like his father treated him. Why he avoided making friends.

She had tried to get a social worker to help Chuck and his family. But they didn't want her help. There was nothing the school could do. Nothing she could do.

Seeing Chuck beside her, Ms. Jensen realized that his parents must still be asleep. That is why he was able to join her in the early morning. Good, she thought, I'm glad. And she knew his running with her could help them get closer. Help get rid of some of his frustration and anger. Maybe help him control his temper. And as Dr. L. told her, it could even help with fine tuning. But at least she now understood the reason behind his blowing up. He had to let out all that hate and frustration somewhere...and he couldn't do it at home. She also understood his silence and need to be alone. Even his defiance. They were all symptoms. And as Dr. L. repeatedly said, "Each symptom is an important message once you understand its meaning. Like a secret code." And Ms. Jensen finally understood Chuck's secret code.

She faced her last lap. While passing the forest, she suddenly realized Chuck had disappeared. Once again, only her own tap, tap, tap echoed in the quiet morning air. Alone. Would Chuck return? she wondered. She'd wait and see. Ms. Jensen's heart was flying. She was hopeful. Hopeful as she ran to meet her class.

2

Meeting the Upside-Down Kids in Class

Ms. JENSEN WALKED into her classroom. One quick look and she knew. She knew the kids were all completely out of control. They were high and flying from the sugar and candy they ate last night on Halloween. They were running, jumping, yelling ...going wild. How she hated to deal with them the next day when they were hung over—like drunks.

Right away, Ms. Jensen knew that trying to teach them anything now would be a complete waste of time. So she reached behind her desk, pulled out her guitar and played a loud chord. Then she sat Indian style on the "talking rug"—the rug she used to sit and chat with the kids. And with the guitar resting in her lap, she began playing and singing, "Michael rowed the boat ashore, Hallelujah..." Her soft voice filled the room like gentle arms, touching everyone, calming them, drawing them over to her rug. Drawing them to her!

Chuck remained in his seat. For once, he seemed to be the calmest kid in the class. He had exercised just that morning. And he didn't have candy. No trick or treating for him. So he wasn't hyper. He just watched the other kids settle down on the "talking rug." Thank God they calmed down, he sighed to himself. They had been driving him crazy. His eyes now landed on Amy as he listened to her sing along with Ms. Jensen. Boy, Amy really has a good voice, he thought.

Amy loved to sing. And she loved Ms. Jensen. So she sat close to her. And a smile filled Amy's face. Her sweet voice joined the group of singing Upside-Down Kids. Ms. Jensen nodded to encourage Amy to continue singing. Amy was always so quiet. Unless she sang. She stuttered and mumbled every time she spoke. So she always talked with a hand covering her mouth. Because she tried to hide her clumsy speech. But when Amy sang her voice was clear. No stumbles. No mumbles. Just beautiful clear notes. Amy was happiest when Ms. Jensen played her guitar. The music fine tuned her speech the same way running and exercise seemed to help the other kids.

Hyper-Harry and Funny-Freddie were still running around the room with their arms stretched out like airplane wings. They crashed into desks, each other, and anyone or anything else that came their way. Finally they flew over to the "talking rug." Then they crashed into each other and tumbled onto the floor. A crash landing. They liked it when Ms. Jensen sang, too. They didn't have to do school work. They didn't have to write or see their letters and numbers jump around upside down and backwards. And they didn't have to concentrate or worry about being distracted by everything and anything. Yup, they agreed with Amy. Listening to music and singing were better than class work any old time. That way they didn't make dumb mistakes and feel stupid.

MICHAEL ROWED THE BOAT ASHORE . . .

Bob-the-Fog walked over to Ms. Jensen's rug and stretched out. He felt like he was always in a fog. His mind's filters were broken. He heard too many voices. Too many noises: kids, teachers, cars outside, birds singing. All the sounds bombed his brain at the same time. Important sounds and unimportant ones. They were all equally loud. His mind couldn't filter out unimportant and distracting sounds. As a result, he either heard everything as a scrambled mess or he blocked everything out. And his brain couldn't understand what was being said fast enough. By the time he said "what" once or twice, his brain's computer finally got it when he was lucky. Otherwise nothing at all would sink in.

The music was good. Lots of voices singing. Soft sounds filled the air around Bob. He stretched out on the floor and flipped down his baseball cap over his brown eyes to block out the room's light. Suddenly, he felt calmer, could concentrate better and didn't feel so dizzy anymore. Now he could daydream in peace—with his eyes open but shielded by his "magic" cap.

"The River Jordan..." Ms. Jensen's singing continued onto the next verse. More voices were added now. Anna galloped over to the "talking rug" as if she were a horse. Her blonde pony tail swished back and forth. She missed riding her horse, Lady. So she pretended to gallop and ride whenever she could. And Anna loved to talk. That's why they called her motor-mouth. Singing and talking were easy. But not reading, writing and spelling. Those subjects were dumb, she often said. But really, deep inside Anna felt like she must be the one who was dumb. And ugly, too. On her horse, Anna felt smart and pretty. In control. In fact, just thinking about riding made her feel smarter. She sat tall. Loud and clear, Anna started singing.

Kram-the-Football-Ram heard Anna's confident voice. He moved to the other side of the "talking rug." Why did Anna always have to be the loudest and the first to speak? he wondered. He hated to speak up in class. Sure, he could when he had to. He wasn't like Amy. He didn't mumble. But he didn't have Anna's quickness and confidence either. Then he thought of his reading. Sweat broke out on his brow. Yeah, he mumbled and stumbled when he read. His eyes stuttered, too. It was torture. Pure torture. Especially when he read out loud. Worse than when he was on the football team facing someone twice his size. *Ha!* He smiled. He'd flatten them. He was tough and confident on the field. Then he remembered. One day he had a bloody nose right before the game. No worry. He felt great. Blood covered his white jersey and his gold number 72. When his mother saw it, she almost fainted. Kram just laughed. The other team was shocked by his blood-stained clothes. Crouched on the front line, he knew he was really psyching the other team out. So he loved it. But, he thought, don't ask me to read. Those stupid words and letters jumped around too fast for his eyes and brain to catch. He felt like a fool. I can't be a fool, he thought, I gotta be tough. Tougher and better than any other kid on the field. Tough and good...so no one will ever know I feel like a fool. So I won't even know it myself. I can't let anyone else see how stupid I feel.

Randy-the-Magician moved closer to Kram. Kram was tough, but Randy knew he was also one of the nicest guys around. A good friend to have. Randy nudged Kram with his elbow. When

Kram looked at him, Randy held out a small Snickers bar. Kram shook his head, *no*. He'd already eaten too much candy. For Randy, there was never too much candy. He thought trick-or-treating was invented just for him. He loved going to houses and being given candy. Yum. Randy loved Halloween. He thought it was the best holiday. He'd never forget it. In class, Randy forgot everything. He'd learn things, and then they quickly and completely disappeared. Forgotten. Magically, like Houdini-the-Magician. Randy's mind made all his school work vanish. Poof! But when he reached deep down into his pockets, he could feel his candy that he always hid there. They didn't vanish. Telephone numbers, times tables, even his own brother's name...vanished. But Randy's candy was always there. Magic— Randy knew that he even got lost sometimes on his way home from school. He just couldn't remember directions, either. But then Randy laughed, while thinking: maybe I could leave a trail of candy wrappers to mark my way home. Like Hansel and...oh well, Hansel and somebody else.

The kids sat and sang. Ms. Jensen looked around the class. She truly loved these kids. They were all so different. Sure, they had problems. But they worked very hard. And they were spunky, too, despite their hardships. Then Ms. Jensen's eyes fell on Chuck. As usual, he sat alone in the back of the room. In the shadows. His arms were folded tightly across his chest. Holding himself in check. And keeping everyone else from coming close.

Chuck's eyes stared out the window watching the last oak leaf on the tree. It fluttered. Would it hold on? Could he hold on? Chuck watched that leaf every day. And Ms. Jensen watched Chuck the same way. Had he really run with her that morning? she wondered. Yes, she knew he had. But he hadn't moved any closer to her. And he didn't join the class now. The song ended. The leaf dipped and swayed, but held tightly to the branch. Chuck continued to watch the leaf just as Ms. Jensen continued to watch and wait for Chuck. She hoped that one day he would feel secure enough to let go and join the class. Join her. But she had to be patient. She couldn't burden Chuck with any more pressure. God knows, he had enough.

3

The Journal

EVERY SCHOOL DAY began the same way. Early each morning, before class started, Ms. Jensen ran on the track. And then suddenly, out of the shadows, Chuck would appear. They would nod silently. It was a quiet time. No talking. A time to share only the crisp early air. A time for being with someone, but not feeling you had to talk. They ran. They watched the last few birds fly south. They listened to the cardinals in the woods, knowing they would stay around for the winter. While running, their hearts pumped. Their faces turned red from the cold and the exercise. They felt alive. Alert. Fine tuned. They raced with the wind. And a common bond grew stronger and stronger. You couldn't see it. But it was there. They could feel it. And just before the last lap, Chuck nodded his good-bye and disappeared into the woods.

One morning in class, after the pledge and birthdays were announced over the loud speaker, Ms. Jensen said, "Today we are going to start some new work. Something very, very special."

Groans filled the room.

"What? What?" Bob-the-Fog asked, knowing he missed something.

"Wait a minute." Ms. Jensen said. "All work is not bad. It may feel frustrating and impossible. But with practice and patience, you can succeed at almost anything you're forced to tackle. You just need the confidence to try and the experience of succeeding. Remember, you are going to have jobs some day. And they won't always be easy or fun. So you have to learn how to tackle and enjoy tasks that initially seem difficult and unpleasant. And eventually you will learn how to cope with and even enjoy challenges. Eventually you'll find jobs that you are good at and that you *like* to do."

"There's no job I like to do," Randy said, leaning back in his chair while reaching his hands deep into his pockets. Yup. Candy. He instantly felt reassured. Candy was his tranquilizer.

"I like my job," Ms. Jensen said. "In fact, I love my job. I like working with all of you. I like trying to make your work fun."

"Impossible," Funny-Freddie laughed. "Saying work is fun is like saying Freddy Kreuger's a nice guy." Everyone shivered and giggled. They all knew that Freddy Kreuger was the horror from the nightmare movies.

"I think it's possible," Ms. Jensen said. "But you all have to remember one thing: things you enjoy are often challenging and difficult to master, like football, acting, horseback riding, music, art, medicine. And on and on it goes. But in the end, it's worth it." She then reached into her bag. "I have a gift for each of you."

"Yesss," Randy-the-Magician said, picturing chocolate bars in her bag.

"Special writing books," Ms. Jensen said.

"Booo," the kids jokingly sang out. Ms. Jensen smiled, took a book from her bag and held it up.

"That doesn't look like a real book," Anna said. "How come it's all white?"

Ms. Jensen walked around the room and gave a book to each of the eight Upside-Down Kids. They

were the size of library books, not regular note-
books. The cover was plain white and the inside
pages had lines to lay their writing and thinking
straight.

Ms. Jensen explained, "These books will be your
very own journals. You can name the book anything
you want. And you will be the author. That's why
the book's cover is blank."

"Can we draw pictures in the book?" Randy-the-
Magician asked. He loved art. As you recall, he won
a dinosaur drawing contest in October. His tyrano-
saurus was the best in the school. Randy just loved
to draw and draw. It was one of the few things he
didn't forget how to do.

"Yes, you may draw on the cover. And you might
even want to draw some things on the inside, too,"
Ms. Jensen said. "But this book is mainly for
words."

"Yuck. I hate writing words," Anna moaned. "No
one can read my writing."

"But that's the best part about this book," Ms.
Jensen said. "In this book...writing and spelling
don't count."

"Yesss!" the class chorused happily.

"Punctuation doesn't count."

"Yesss!"

"And you don't have to use complete sentences, either."

"Yesss!"

"This book is for your eyes only."

"*Y e s s s!*" Everyone shouted.

"If no one's gonna see it, we don't have to write nothin'," Hyper-Harry whispered.

But Ms. Jensen heard. She smiled, "Yes, Harry, you will write. I'll check on that. But it doesn't matter what or how you write. We'll all think of lots of fun ideas to write about. And you won't be marked wrong for mistakes. Mistakes don't count in this book."

"Horses," Anna said. "Let's write about horses."

Kram groaned, "All you ever think about is horses."

"So," Anna shot back, "all you ever talk about is football!"

"Anna," Ms. Jensen said, breaking up their fight. Anna and Kram loved to argue. A typical lovers' quarrel. "Anna, what day is today?" Ms. Jensen continued.

"Monday."

"Good. And what is the date?"

"November eighth," Anna shouted before anyone else could answer. Then she sat back in her chair and pouted. Why do I always talk so much? she thought. I always talk first. Out loud. Motor-Mouth they call me...and they're right. Anna slumped down in her seat. She didn't like that name, but she couldn't stop talking, either. Her mother called her *impulsive*. Because she couldn't control her mouth. That was true, she decided. But then she thought, it's better to speak up. That way you sometimes sounded smart. When she wrote, she felt like her writing looked dumb! Some letters were big. Some small. Some backwards. Dumb. Dumb. Dumb. She held her pencils so tightly that they actually broke. Yup, she thought, I'd rather speak than write. "Yes, it's Monday, November eighth. Friday's my birthday. And my name's gonna be on the loud speaker—as if I were already a famous movie star. And we're gonna have a party—to celebrate my winning an Academy Award. Or a horse riding contest. We're going to have chocolate cupcakes with chocolate icing and

M&M's on top so that each looks like a happy face."

"Yummm," Randy-the-Magician grinned, almost tasting the cupcakes. "I'll be your best friend," he smiled, thinking he might get two.

Oh no, Ms. Jensen thought, no more sugar. But instead Ms. Jensen said, "Anna, I'm glad you know the date. Now will you please come up here and write it on the board?"

Anna froze. All the pink color drained out of her face. "N...no," she mumbled, shaking her head. Her pony tail flipped from side to side, like a horse trying to break free from a coral. "Not write. Not on the board. I can't."

"Sure you can, Anna. I'll help you." Ms. Jensen took Anna's hand and led her to the chalkboard. "First we'll just make the letters big in the air. All of you kids could improve your penmanship by writing in the air. Everyone, take your writing hand and hold it out in front of you."

Ms. Jensen was trying to get the Upside-Down Kids to feel their writing movements with their big muscles as well as those in their hands. Often, dyslexic kids can't remember the movements needed to write legibly when using only their fingers and hands. And visualizing the movements and directions needed to write helped klutzy writers like Anna compensate even more.

Ms. Jensen stood behind Anna and put her right hand over Anna's hand. She asked, "What letter does Monday begin with?"

"M," Anna whispered.

"Good. Everyone close your eyes and draw an *M* in the air. As if you were writing on a big magic blackboard. Down, around and down, around and down. Good. What is the next letter in Monday?"

"O."

"Yes. Now I want you all to picture a large clock in the air in front of you. Eyes still closed. Now reach out. Put your hand on the 2. Good. Now go from the 2 back to 12. Around to 2."

Randy opened his eyes. "Hey, that's a neat way to make a circle."

"Yes," Ms. Jensen agreed. "Now for the *n*. Like the *M*. Down, around and down. Oops, wrong way, Anna. Let me hold your hand. Down, around and down. Away from you. Yes, that's it." Ms. Jensen had the kids picture a clock and the numbers on it. This

would help them remember how to draw the letters and their directions in space. Klutzy writers often forget these single movement patterns just like klutzy people who often trip forget where to put their feet when they're walking and running. "Now the *d* is a small clock with a handle. Remember, 2 back to 12. Around to 4. Up through the 2. Overhead and down."

Up and down. That was all Hyper-Harry and Funny-Freddie needed to hear. With their eyes closed they jumped out of their seats reaching for the ceiling. Then they crashed back down into their chairs. Ms. Jensen ignored them. She went right to the *a*.

"Hand on the 2. Back to 12. Around to 4. Up to 1. Down to 4. Good. Keep doing the a's in the air until you feel good about them."

"Do we have to do the whole word, November?" Kram asked.

"No. We'll abbreviate it. *N*. Down around and down. Now the clock again. Hand on the 2. Back to 12. Around to 2. Good. *V*. Down and up. Easy. You're all doing super," Ms. Jensen said. She watched Harry's hand doing all sorts of extra flip flops in the air, but he was still trying. When writing, his hand and pencil were like mixed-up drunken missiles trying to follow and hit a moving target.

"For the 8, we can just put one clock on top of another," Freddie said. He was smart enough to imagine simple designs for letters and numbers he could follow with his mind when his missile-hand was steering him off course.

"Wonderful," Ms. Jensen smiled. "Everyone, please open your journals. Anna will be putting the date on the board now. And I want you all to write it down in your books. First page, top line. Every day we'll start with the day and the date," Ms. Jensen said while guiding Anna's hand in writing Monday, Nov. 8. Anna stepped back and looked at her work. "Wow," she grinned. "That's the neatest I ever wrote. That clock stuff really works." By using her big muscles and mind's eye, she was able to correct for the steering difficulties she had in her missile-hand when writing. That was a first for her. Anna wanted to get back to her seat and write the date in her journal. Neatly. Everyone carefully copied the date.

Chuck stared out the window as if he was ignoring everything. But when Ms. Jensen walked around the room, she saw that Chuck already had the date written in his book. She nodded approvingly to him as she passed his desk, just like she did out on the running track. Chuck often didn't write anything. Maybe this was a new beginning for him. Just maybe.

"But what are we going to write about?" Randy-the-Magician asked. He looked at the blank page in front of him. It was like his magic had already made the words on the paper disappear. Then he smiled, "Hey, I wish I could really be a magician and just snap my fingers and make words appear. That'd be a good trick. Then I'd be a right-side-up Houdini instead of a dyslexic one."

"Yeah, me too," Anna nodded. Kram agreed also. Anna and Kram smiled at each other. They finally agreed on something.

"Do you all remember when we were studying mammals in science?" Ms. Jensen asked.

"What?" Bob-the-Fog asked.

"Yes, I do," Freddie-the-Clown said. "And the Woolly Mammoth was the largest land mammal that ever lived. It looked like an elephant, but was twice as big. And it had long brown hair that hung down to the ground." Freddie stood. He bent over, grabbing his hands together in front of him. He swung his arms like an elephant's trunk.

"Yes, that's right, Freddie. That's just what he looked like," Ms. Jensen joked, watching Freddie move slowly around like an elephant. "Well, today you are going to write..." She began. Then she turned to the board and wrote, "If I were a Woolly Mammoth..." The class copied her words. She said, "Use your imaginations. Where would you live? Use your senses. What would you see around you? What sounds would you hear? Would you have friends? What would you eat?"

"I'd eat my friends," Randy joked. Everyone laughed.

"Tell me about the best thing and the worst thing that could happen to you," Ms. Jensen added.

"Being eaten by your friends," Anna joked, grabbed her throat and pretended to choke. Everyone in the class liked to kid around. It was easier to make fun than to be made fun of. And they were all used to being made fun of. Ms. Jensen understood that. By now, the kids did, too.

"Begin writing," Ms. Jensen said to the kids. And she pulled out one more white book from her bag for herself. "I'll write, too."

"Y... you, too?" Amy questioned, surprised to see her teacher do class work. Ms. Jensen nodded, yes.

"And spelling doesn't count?" Kram asked, not quite believing that could be true.

"Right. Spelling doesn't count."

"What? No one's gonna read it?" Bob-the-Fog asked, not quite sure he heard correctly.

"Right. No one's going to read it."

"But we can read it out loud if we want?" Funny-Freddie asked. "Mine's gonna be really good. Really funny."

"We'll see," Ms. Jensen said. "But no one will *have* to show their writing to others. Now, no more stalling questions. Write." Ms. Jensen knew the kids were asking questions for two reasons. To make sure they weren't going to be tricked and made to feel stupid. And to kill more time before being forced to write.

A busy quiet fell over the room. Pencils raced across paper. Not having to worry about neatness and spelling made everyone feel free to write what they wanted to and not just words that they could spell. Time passed. All the kids wondered to themselves, why hadn't any other teacher tried to help them this way before? Hadn't they cared enough? Didn't they know enough? Were they just mean? Or stupid, or both? Were they upside-down teachers?

4

Calculators and Computers

DURING THAT WEEK, every day began with journal writing. The things that they wrote about were fun. Tuesday they wrote about the best thing that ever happened to them. Wednesday was the worst thing. Thursday was about their best vacation. But they really liked Friday's question the best: If you could be any animal in the world for one day, what animal would you be?

After the writing time, Funny-Freddie jumped out of his seat. "Please let me read mine. It's great. But I'm not gonna tell what animal I am. You have to guess."

Ms. Jensen grinned. "Freddie, you're one step ahead of me. I was just going to ask if anyone wanted to share their writing with the class."

Freddie raced to the front of the room. His face was red with excitement. And the red filled in all the spaces between his freckles. He began writing on the chalkboard. The big arm movements Ms. Jensen used to form letters really helped Freddie write more clearly. Less klutzy. Now he felt proud that he could read what he had written. Excitedly he told the class, "It's a poem. The kind that doesn't rhyme."

"Free verse," Anna said, always ready to help out whether anyone wanted help or not.

"Yeah. Whatever," Freddie said, "here goes:

If I were a

blank

I'd be sleek

Sneaky and black.

There wouldn't be a

Spot or a freckle on me.

I'd hide in shadows

And pounce on my prey.

No one would be safe

With me around.

I'd eat you and you
And YOU!"

Freddie shouted the last word and pointed at everyone.

"I know. I know," Hyper-Harry shouted, jumping up. "A black panther. A black panther."

"Yup. Yup. You're..." choke...gasp. Suddenly Freddie, after being so excited, couldn't catch his breath. Choking, he gasped for air. All color left his face. Even his freckles turned white. Freddie was scared. So were the other kids. They had seen Freddie choke before, but never this bad.

Ms. Jensen put an arm around Freddie's shoulder. While trying to calm him, she led him out to the hall. "Breathe slowly," she instructed. "Inhale deeply. And hold your breath. Then let it out slowly." Freddie's wheezing slowed. After he seemed better, Ms. Jensen asked Hyper-Harry to take his friend, Freddie, to the nurse. Maybe the school doctor would see him, too. She thought Freddie's wheezing might be due to allergies. That would also explain why he always looked so pale and tired and black around the eyes. Also, Freddie said he had nightmares. So maybe he couldn't sleep. Yes, she thought, Dr. L. could probably help Freddie a great deal with his nightmares and dyslexia. And maybe even his allergies, too.

When Ms. Jensen walked back into the room, she saw Anna in command of the class. While standing in front of the kids just like a teacher, Anna said, "I'm gonna read 'bout my animal. Okay?" The class was quiet. The kids had learned to control themselves in Ms. Jensen's class. They knew she really, really cared about them. So they cared about her. And they did things for her that they never did for any other teacher. They listened and tried their best.

"Continue Anna," Ms. Jensen nodded.

"Okay, you guys," Anna said, "Listen up. You have to guess what animal I am."

"Bet I know," Kram said while getting on all fours, raising his head and whinnying. He knew the only animals Anna ever talked about were horses.

"Ssssh. Wait," Anna demanded. "No one can guess 'til I'm done. Okay. Here goes:

If I were a
blank
I'd see fields and fences
And green grass
I'd hear wind whistling in my ears.
I'd race by so fast
You'd think I was flying.
I'd eat grass, hay, carrots and
Sugar cubes (If I was lucky).
The best would be having someone who
Loved me, cared for me, and rode me.
The worst would be feeling ugly
And all alone."

Every hand was up beating the air. Except Chuck's. Maybe he listened. But it didn't look that way. His eyes were still glued to the leaf on the tree outside. It was like he was magically holding it there, just by wishing it not to fall off. Just like he was forcing himself to hold on—by sheer will power.

"Me. Me. Pick me," Randy shouted. "I'll be your best friend."

Silent-Amy had her hand up. Anna knew that

Amy almost never raised her hand to speak out loud in class. So Anna swung her arm over everyone's head. Finally, her arm stopped and pointed at Amy.

Amy knew the answer. However, when she saw Anna pointing at her, Amy felt a lump jump up in her throat. She quickly put her hand over her mouth and forced out the word, "H...horse."

"You're absolutely right," Anna shouted as if Amy had answered a difficult million-dollar question.

"That was easy," Bob-the-Fog said. "I even knew it."

"That was very good, Anna," Ms. Jensen said. "I'm so pleased that you and Freddie were able to write about things you sense. Things you hear, eat, and feel. You also used something that made me feel good. You remembered to use *alliteration* in your poems. That great big word I just said means words near each other in a sentence that begin with the same letter. Anna, I think you said 'fences and fields.'" Ms. Jensen said.

Anna looked at her and smilingly said, "And 'green grass,' and 'wind whistling.'"

"Excellent. I also liked the end of your poem, when the horse didn't wants to feel ugly and alone. Just like you kids feel. No one wants to feel ugly and alone. And no one should just because you have dyslexia. Just because you're different. And special. That doesn't make you ugly or stupid. That shouldn't get you rejected. Feeling alone."

The class was quiet. Hyper-Harry and Freddie-the-Clown were back from the nurse. Every one of the eight kids often felt ugly, stupid and alone. Especially when they tried to do things that were hard for them. Things that were easy for others. Even pretty Anna felt ugly and stupid. Different. Anna wondered, without riding a horse, how do you feel good? How do you feel special? She wondered if she would ever feel good about herself *all* the time. Especially in school.

During the next two months, so many new things happened to the Upside-Down Kids in class that they often felt like their heads were spinning around like tops. Ms. Jensen invited Dr. L., the doctor who helped treat her own dyslexia, to come and speak to the class. The kids asked Dr. L. many interesting questions.

"Dr. L.," Anna asked first, "if dyslexia is mainly when people have trouble reading, how come I also have trouble writing?"

"Good question, Anna," Dr. L. said. "Many people think dyslexia is only when letters and words they read reverse. But it is many other things, too. Dyslexia may scramble or mess up the way you write. Or how you speak. Or it may make you hyper and klutzy and confused about directions such as right and left. Dyslexia could also make it difficult to remember things, like numbers or math, telling time or following directions. And very often people with dyslexia will have nightmares and fears."

"Why? Why do they have nightmares and fears?" Freddie-the-Clown asked, remembering his own terrible nightmares about drowning.

"People have nightmares and fears for many, many reasons," Dr. L. answered. "Very often, nightmares express the worries and fears we feel during the day, but keep to ourselves, and even hide from ourselves. For example, if kids feel overloaded or overwhelmed during the day because of their school problems, they might express this terrible feeling by dreaming they were choking, unable to catch

41

their breath or drowning. In kids who feel off balance and dizzy during the day or even at night while sleeping, they might dream of floating or falling from a height. In fact, these same kids might fear falling from heights during the day, as well. Kids who get motion sick in cars or planes or when overloaded in crowded places might also develop fears of moving elevators, planes or buses. Even crowd fears—in movies, department stores, busy subways, and libraries. Kids who have difficulty learning might become frightened of school or classes or even homework assignments. Some may panic at the thought of going to class. And kids who have difficulty speaking might become self-conscious—and avoid speaking in front of others."

"So why are we different?" Kram said. "Why are we dumb?"

Dr. L. smiled. "Yes, dyslexics are different. But they certainly aren't dumb! They have been among the greatest minds that ever lived. Albert Einstein, Thomas Edison, Woodrow Wilson, Winston Churchill, Leonardo da Vinci were all different and dyslexic. There certainly wasn't too much wrong with their brains. And if there was, I'd love to have their problem. And so would you. A great scientist once said, 'Dyslexia is nature's way of creating a new and wonderful society.' Do you know why? Because these are the people who will have to work harder. More creatively. They must try, try, try and never give up. They must be determined. To succeed with dyslexia, they often discover and do many new and wonderful things. Different, yes. Dumb, never.

"In fact, I'll let you in on a little secret I found out after examining thousands of Upside-Down Kids just like you. The smarter they were, the more frustrated they got. And the dumber they felt. Really dumb kids don't expect anything from themselves. No one else does either. So they don't really feel as frustrated or dumb as bright kids.

"You can also talk a really dumb kid into thinking they're a genius like Einstein. But bright kids can't be talked into anything. They won't believe it when you tell them the truth, that they're bright— even when they're super bright and gifted. They think you're just trying to make them feel better. Brighter.

"There are only two ways to make a bright kid feel as bright as he really is. First, you have to explain to him scientifically or medically why he has every single symptom he has and how he got that way. Once dyslexic kids have a true understanding of why they are the way they are, they won't blame themselves so much for their failures. They won't feel so guilty anymore. They won't believe a lot of foolish things people tell them. For example, so-called experts often mistakenly blame kids or their parents for the symptoms. These experts even think dyslexic kids complain of their symptoms only because they want attention. And that they would be symptom-free if only they weren't so lazy and tried harder.

"There's also a second way you get dyslexic kids to feel better about themselves. Once they are able to accomplish and succeed, and once their symptoms decrease or disappear, they immediately feel better about themselves. They no longer feel stupid, ugly, lazy, crazy...

"This is why it's so important to have teachers like Ms. Jensen. She can help you learn better—differently. In fact, I've lots of patients with dyslexia who have graduated from Harvard, Yale, and Princeton. Some got help and others did it entirely on their own. They all found ways to get around their problems. That's why it's so very important that you know of all the educational and medical ways that can help you reach your full potential. And even why these different methods work when they do.

"In fact, before this term is over, I am sure Ms. Jensen will inform you and your parents about all the different methods around that can really help."

Dr. L. continued, "Now I'd like to ask you all a question. And I'd like you to figure out the answer by yourselves. I'm sure you've all noticed that running, exercises and gymnastics often make you feel better—less dyslexic. Can you guess why? You needn't tell me now. Just think about it and we can discuss it at a later date."

Suddenly Anna raised her hand and had an answer on the tip of her tongue. For the same reason the medications do, she thought. But before she said anything, the whole class started laughing. They weren't laughing at Anna. They all knew that Anna had figured out the answer at lightning speed—as always. Even Anna started laughing, too. She couldn't help it. Her thinking and speaking were as fast as her reading and writing were slow.

"Hold your answer 'til later," Dr. L. gently told Anna. "Let's see if the rest of you kids can figure out reasons of your own. And write them in your books. Then Ms. Jensen will discuss them all with you."

Anna was not insulted at all by Dr. L. putting her off. She quickly understood the importance of getting everyone to think things out for themselves. However, she didn't yet realize that Dr. L. was also trying to get her to control her impulsive speech.

Anna held her answer. But with a whimsical smile, she asked Dr. L. a few amazing questions:

"Dr. L., you told us last time Ms. Jensen invited you to our class that there's something wrong with our inner ears. And that there are medications that can help us. Can you explain it to us again? Can you help us get better?"

"After examining thousand of kids just like you and even adults like Ms. Jensen, I discovered that the only thing wrong with dyslexics is that they have a simple inner ear problem.

"The inner ear acts as a fine tuner to the brain. And when there's a problem, the visual and hearing signals coming into the brain often become blurry or scrambled or twisted. And the same thing happens to the balance and coordination signals going out. That explains your reading symptoms. And even why Bob has difficulty hearing things clearly and rapidly and why Harry often trips and falls.

"In fact, I found that I could make anyone dyslexic by spinning them around long enough. Then they'd get dizzy, develop headaches, and feel off balance and clumsy. Their minds would feel fuzzy and they'd have trouble concentrating and remembering. Their eyes would bounce around so they wouldn't be able to read straight. And they'd begin to write, talk, and move like a drunk—like a dyslexic. In other words, the spinning would scramble a person's fine tuner—just like the scrambled fine tuners of a dyslexic. And special medications and vitamins reset and retune these scrambled fine tuners so they function normally. And guess what? Even astronauts can become dyslexic in space. That's why they're given the same medications that I give people with dyslexia. It really, really helps them most of the time."

The kids liked and easily understood that answer. Many in the class then went to visit Dr. L. at his office. He had special medical tests he gave to figure out what was wrong with them. And as a result of these medical tests, Dr. L. found them all to have the same inner-ear problem he told them about. Both the kids and their parents were relieved. For the first time ever, they had an answer. For the first time ever, they had an understanding of what was wrong and what to do about it. They couldn't wait to begin treatment.

Dr. L. put Randy on medicine to help his memory. Amy was treated to help with her speech coordination and difficulties with math. Harry was given medicine for his hyperactivity. Interestingly, Dr. L. found that Freddie was recently given similar medicine for his allergies and asthma. And so he was also beginning to do much better in spelling. And he seemed better coordinated, too. In addition to medicine, Bob-the-Fog was given blue-tinted glasses that helped to cut out the glare of flourescent and other lights in school. These lights made him

anxious and distracted. Both the medicine and the glasses helped him read and concentrate better. Eye exercises and games like Nintendo were also recommended to help the kids with their eye tracking. So they wouldn't lose their place so much when reading. And Harry-the-Klutz was also given special balance and coordination exercises in order to improve his reflexes and to keep him from tripping and falling all the time. Last but not least, Anna and Kram were treated for their reading, writing and spelling problems. And hopefully, Anna's speech-impulsivity or motor mouth would improve as well.

After a few weeks of treatment, Dr. L. returned to the class. That's when Bob asked Dr. L., "Why do the blue glasses help me to see the words clearly?"

"Great, great question, Bob. Most people, and even experts, aren't sure of the answer. But let me tell you in a simple way what I've found out. Do you remember Ms. Jensen and I explained to the class that dyslexics often have 'holes' in their filters. That's why they frequently hear sounds they shouldn't hear, or are distracted by moving things they shouldn't see. Even odors that others don't smell. Some even feel things on their skin too much.

That's why they're sensitive to tight-fitting clothes and even being touched. And others are very sensitive to motion.

"If your eyes are letting in too much light, then sunglasses will help cut down on the light getting in your eyes. Have any of you experienced too much sunlight in your eyes? That's the way some kids feel when their 'light filter' is broken. Others have broken sound, touch, smell, and even broken motion filters. The medications I use can help fix these filters from the inside. And the colored glasses help the visual filter from the outside."

Ms. Jensen then added, "Don't expect medicines and glasses to fix everything. Dyslexics still have to study and work very, very hard. That's why teachers are so important. They can teach you simple ways to learn—simple ways to get around your problem. And they can help you catch up and relearn all the things you missed—even after the medicines begin to work.

Then one day after Dr. L's visit to the class, Ms. Jensen opened a new box in front of the eight kids. "I'd like you all to meet SR," she said. I think you are really going to like having SR in class.

How many in here have trouble spelling words?"

Grumbles filled the room. "Well, then you will love SR. The name means Spell-Right. SR for short. We'll put him over in the corner. If you are not sure how to spell a word, all you have to do is type in how you think it is spelled. And SR will give you the correct spelling."

Anna placed her hands over her heart. "SR, I think I love you."

"You mean we can use SR instead of a diction-ary?" Randy asked.

"Sure," Ms. Jensen said. "It's very difficult to use the dictionary, especially when you have trouble remembering the letters and the spelling sounds."

"You can say that again," Freddie agreed. "'Cause you start looking up the end or the middle of a word instead of the beginning. And sometimes you begin with a letter from another word. And you wind up frustrated—in outer space."

"It is very difficult..." Ms. Jensen repeated, joking. The class laughed. SR became a very impor-tant part of the class.

Then the next week, Ms. Jensen brought in a few calculators. She placed them around the room.

Harry, who always hated math and had so many problems with numbers, wanted to spend the whole day playing with the calculator. And Magic-Randy now had a reliable memory-chip for numbers, too, which he could use when his magic erased those in his head. If only he could find some other chips to help him remember all the other facts he lost. Perhaps Dr. L. would help.

Finally, the week before Thanksgiving, the kids decided to prepare a feast in class. They wrote out recipe cards for the foods they liked the best. They used their calculators to figure out how to double and triple the amounts needed in the recipes. And at the end of the party, Ms. Jensen packaged all the extra food left over. Then she caught Chuck just before he left. "Chuck," she spoke softly, "please bring this home. For your mom."

"We don't need no charity," he grumbled, his face turning red.

"No. Of course not. But this isn't charity. This is just the leftover food we made. I can't see it going to waste. I'm flying to Boston for the weekend, so I can't take it with me. I hoped you could help me out by taking it home."

"Well, uh, okay. Just to help you out. Uh, thanks," Chuck mumbled and slipped out the door with the huge bag of food under his arm. It would be the only Thanksgiving food he would have. Ms. Jensen knew that. She wanted to help Chuck, but she knew she had to be very careful not to embarrass him.

By the beginning of December, the kids found out about Ms. Jensen and Chuck running together every morning. One dark morning, Anna and Kram showed up and joined them. Chuck glared. He hated them breaking up this special time. But he knew he was just part of the class—one in eight. Chuck glared at Anna and warned, "No talkin.'"

Huffing and puffing her way around the track, Anna gasped, "No problem!" Running made it easy to control her talking. She couldn't run and speak at the same time. I'm gonna be the first woman president, she thought. She remembered that President Ford was dyslexic and he couldn't chew gum and walk at the same time. I'll make Harry-the-Klutz my vice president cause he can't walk even without chewing gum.

The next day, Randy-the-Magician and Bob-the-Fog came to school at 6:15 A.M. Randy shivered.

"I've gotta be crazy. It's not even light out. I could be home in my nice warm bed...or eating a huge breakfast. French toast. Bacon. Juice." At the thought of food, Randy's eyes glazed over. He could almost taste the maple syrup in his mouth and feel it running down his chin. Huffing and gasping, he slid his tongue over his lips, hoping to really, really taste it.

"Yeah, this is crazy," Funny-Freddie and Hyper-Harry agreed, arriving out of breath but overhearing what Randy was saying.

"Nobody asked ya to come," Chuck sneered. He was mad. But he was determined not to be driven away by the other kids. "Oh no," Chuck groaned, seeing Amy slowly walk around the corner.

"H... hi," she smiled nervously.

Everyone ran together as a group. But Chuck decided not to remain with the pack. So he quickened his pace and ran twice as fast as everyone else. He still couldn't take the chance of getting too close to the other kids. But Ms. Jensen got to him. And so did the others. That's why he couldn't run away from the rest of the class, although he felt trapped by his feelings. But not as scared or angry as before. He almost liked the feeling of belonging to the class. Almost!

Suddenly, Freddie started wheezing. Ms. Jensen stopped running and went right over to him. "Don't feel bad, Freddie," she said. "Running isn't for everyone. Especially in the winter. Take a break. You might want to try it again in the spring."

Freddie agreed. But the rest of the Upside-Down Kids stayed with the jogging. Soon it wasn't that they were running as a group, or a class. They were running for themselves. They set their own pace. They set their own rhythm. They began to feel good about themselves as they saw their pace and rhythm improve. Most of the kids lived close enough to school so that they could go home, shower, and eat before class started. The kids that lived far away showered in the gym and ate in the cafeteria. Before long, most of the kids liked to start their day this way—by jogging first.

Once in their classroom, they got right to their journals. They helped make up fun questions to write about. Scary moments. Fears. Worst vacations. They all liked writing when they didn't have to worry about penmanship and spelling words right.

They wrote more and more all the time. A pattern was forming. A rhythm. The class quieted down. They worked better and better.

One day Ms. Jensen asked the class, "Do you feel better running?"

They all shouted, "Yes."

"Have you all figured out why?"

"Sure," Anna said. "Do you all want to know?"

"Yes," the class said.

"Then I'll get the answer from Dr. L." Anna replied. "But I know what he's going to say. He's going to say that running helps your fine tuning. Just like the medication. That's why they spin and turn astronauts so hard before space flights. To strengthen their filters and fine turners.

Ms. Jensen was amazed at what Anna said. And so was the rest of the class. Even Chuck. She then asked the other kids what they had figured out and written in their journals.

Suddenly, they all started laughing. And together they read the same answer that Anna first gave. Ask Dr. L.

Before the end of the year, Ms. Jensen wheeled a computer into the classroom. It had a color screen and a printer.

"Games," Freddie yelled.

"Yes," Ms. Jensen agreed, "but much more."

"Can I type my stories on it?" Anna asked, touching the keys.

"Yes, you may."

"I'm in love," she swooned.

"Not again," Kram grumbled. "You sure fall in love easy! Even with a computer?"

Ms. Jensen explained. "The computer also has a way to check and correct spelling errors, just like SR. And it always writes very neatly no matter how bad your penmanship is. It's so easy to fix your mistakes without having to rewrite the page over and over again."

Anna couldn't wait to sit down and get to writing.

Ms. Jensen looked at her class. They had come a long way since the beginning of the year. Randy was losing weight with the early runs on the track. Harry and Randy had both calmed down with Dr. L.'s inner-ear medications. Amy had stopped stuttering so much. And even her speech therapist said she was doing much better—except when she got nervous. Freddie's allergies were clearing up. He also looked more rested. No doubt his nightmares were ending. Bob loved his tinted glasses almost as much as his baseball cap. He acted like he was Michael Jackson half the time and a baseball player the other half. And Kram was wild about the second SR Ms. Jensen gave him. He used it all the time. She knew Anna was happy with the new computer. And as if by magic, many of the kids' symptoms started to disappear.

But Ms. Jensen's emotions were upside down over Chuck. Her eyes misted whenever she looked at him. She knew the running he did was good. And so did he. He was always there at the track. Even if it was cold and rainy. Even if all the other kids stayed home. But Chuck still remained apart from everyone in class. Will I be able to reach out and hold him? she wondered. His life was so troubled and hard. She continually prayed he'd make it. That would be her best Christmas present ever. All the kids were excited about Christmas and Chanukah now. But she knew there would be no Christmas for Chuck.

After the holidays, Ms. Jensen had an exciting

project for the class. It would be different. And it involved them working together in groups of two. She thought it would be good for the kids to share their efforts with one another. What she didn't know was just how great the kids were going to do.

Ms. Jensen prayed Chuck would become a part of her new class project. She didn't want to lose him. Not now. Not after all the effort Chuck had made to control his temper and to remain in class. Not after he overcame his fears sufficiently to continue running with her and the class. He was trying his best even if it didn't look that way to the others. If only he would succeed!

5

Welcome Mr. B

THIS WAS THE MESSAGE Ms. Jensen had written on the board. It greeted the eight Upside-Down Kids when they walked into class after vacation. They knew it was their journal entry. It was back to work for them. But everyone was too excited to begin right away. They wanted to talk about their holidays. Besides, it was snowing. And the kids always loved a snowy day. Especially when it was the first snow of the year. Giggling and laughing, the Upside-Down Kids shook wet snow off their clothes. They couldn't run today. And they had half hoped school would be closed so they couldn't work. But it seemed that their school *never* closed for a snowy day. For the first time ever, they really didn't mind returning to school after a holiday. This new feeling shocked them all.

"Hey look," Kram called, pulling his own Spell-Right out of his back pocket. "Here, Ms. Jensen. You can have yours back. Thanks. I've got my own now."

"Me too," Anna grinned, pulling one out of her new purple backpack.

"Oh no. Not again," Kram groaned, rolling his eyes up to the ceiling. "You always have what I have ...or do what I do. Always."

"Wait. Me too," Funny-Freddie shouted, holding up his SR.

Randy-the-Magician called, "Hey guys, look what I got for Chanukah."

"An SR," Kram groaned, pretending to be disgusted.

"Nope. A calculator," Randy grinned.

"Me too," Hyper-Harry said, holding up his new calculator. But he wasn't as hyper as before. There was something different about him.

"I think I must be in a class of Whiz-Kids," Ms. Jensen smiled. "You are all going to be so smart. As smart as you really are."

"I went skiing with my brother," Bob-the-Fog said, making a weird face. Everyone knew Bob and his older brother Tim didn't get along. Tim always teased Bob and beat him up whenever he could.

"Was it really bad?" Randy asked, worried. Randy knew what Bob was going through. He also had problems with his own brother.

Bob smiled. "Not bad at all. Really. I got pretty good at skiing this time. In fact, it seemed pretty easy. I think all the running this fall really helped. Sometimes Tim even had to race to keep up with me. It was great."

"L...look," Amy said in her sweet tiny voice. She hardly ever spoke so all the kids came over to see what she had. Then with both hands, she pulled out a shiny blue box with pink flowers on the side. On the top stood a little ballerina doll balanced on one leg. Her hair was long and brown, just like Amy's. Amy turned a key on the bottom of the box. Music played. The ballerina doll suddenly began moving its arms over its head and spinning slowly around.

"That's beautiful," Anna said. "Do you know

the words to the song, Amy?"

Amy nodded, yes.

"Would you sing them for us?" Anna asked.

Amy turned white. Although she didn't stutter when she sang, she was still nervous every time she opened her mouth in front of others. She looked around at her classmates. Would they make fun of her? Laugh? Then her eyes landed on Chuck. He was staring directly at her. What does his stare mean? she wondered. His eyes were so dark, you couldn't tell what he was thinking. Chuck nodded, yes. He wanted her to sing. That nod gave her the extra courage she needed. Amy listened to the music for a minute then joined in. "Dance bal-ler-i-na, dance..."

After a minute or two, the music stopped. And so did Amy. Suddenly, everyone started clapping. Amy blushed.

"I want to learn that song," Anna begged Amy. "Will you teach me?"

A smile lit up Amy's face. "S...sure. I'll t... teach you," Amy said. Although she still stuttered and hesitated, there was something different about the way she spoke. Better. Amy looked at Chuck. He didn't smile, but he did give her another nod. Amy knew that nod meant, good job. She smiled back at Chuck, but he was already staring out the window. Amy noticed his leaf was still there. Even with the snow on the branch, the oak leaf was still holding on. She hoped it would never fall off. That the tree would never lose it. It was almost as if the class would lose Chuck when the tree lost that last leaf. Amy didn't want to lose Chuck. She and Chuck never spoke. But somehow Amy knew if she ever needed anything, Chuck would be there for her. Maybe it was that they both were quiet. She felt like they shared a special bond. Maybe Chuck would be stronger than the leaf he stared at. Just maybe he'd hold onto the rest of the kids and Ms. Jensen when the leaf fell. That was Amy's secret New Year's wish.

"Okay. Okay," Ms. Jensen called, "let's settle down. I know it's a little harder today with the snow and the holidays. I know you're all happy to see each other. And so happy to be back in school. So we'll get right to work."

"Ugh!" Groans and moans filled the room as everyone moved back to their desks. They took out their journals.

"Bob," Ms. Jensen explained, "I've added this three-sided screen around your desk. You mentioned that other sounds and movements disturbed you. Try this. See if you like it. It may help your eye and ear filters work better."

Bob-the-Fog sat down. He looked at the walls around him and tried writing. Suddenly he started losing his breath. Gasping, he grabbed for his throat. His eyes widened. "No!" he shouted, jumping up. "No walls. They close me in. I can't stand it." He had that same feeling before when trapped in small, crowded places. His father had the same problem, too. Although he couldn't recall the name exactly, it sounded something like cl...claust...

"No problem," Ms. Jensen said and quickly removed the screen from around Bob's desk. "Dr. L. has a name for the way you feel when surrounded by the screen. Claustrophobia. And guess what? He can simply explain it to you—and he can treat it, too. But just in case he forgets to tell you about it, let me tell you what I've learned. You all know what happens when your broken filters let in too much light, or noise, or motion? Dr. L. has already explained that.

"But he left out what happens when your filters block out too much light and sound. People get just as anxious and upset when *over*loaded as when *under*loaded, when their minds don't get enough of a load. That's what we call claustrophobia. It's like being locked up in jail all by yourself—with nothing to see or hear. Running out lets you see and hear and feel all the things your mind needs to function normally. Just like someone starving and dying to eat."

"I want the screen. I want it," Randy called. "Maybe I'll make like Houdini and disappear behind it."

"Fine," Ms. Jensen jokingly said. And she moved the screen around Randy.

This was great, Randy-the-Magician thought. Dr. L. had put him on medication. But he was told to watch what he ate—especially colored candy and chocolate. That made him hyper—and spacy, too. Randy laughed. He always watched everything he ate! He watched it move from his hand to his mouth. Now with this screen, he could sneak food out of his pocket and into his mouth. Yeah, he decided, he was going to like this screen lots.

Just then the door to the room opened and a huge guy walked in. His hair was short and stood straight up—a crew cut. Kram noticed everything about him right away. His neck was huge and his arms were bulging with muscles. Randy peeked over the screen to see him better.

"Great. Here you are. Class," Ms. Jensen called, getting everyone's attention, "I'd like you to meet Mr. Battlelione. Mr. Battlelione will be doing his student teaching with us. He'll spend the rest of the year helping us. And we will help him become a super teacher."

Anna was going crazy. He was gorgeous. And he'd be with them all year. She was in love again. "Mr. Battle...Mr. Battlei...Mr. B. How about it if we call you Mr. B.?" For the first time in her life, Anna couldn't say what she wanted to. At first she thought it was a medication symptom. Dr. L. told them all to blame the medications first for whatever went wrong. Then she smiled and shook her head, No. It's not the medicine. It's *love.* She was too excited to speak.

Mr. B.'s voice was deep and low. "Great. You can call me Mr. B.," he said, smiling at Anna.

Anna swooned. What a smile, she thought. Her heart raced. Yup, she was definitely in love. And for the first time in her life, she thought that going to school was great. And that it would be getting better and better. It wasn't only Mr. B. that made her feel good, she thought. Somehow her reading and writing were getting better, too. The words were getting easier to read and write. Her missile-eyes and -hands were much more on target. And her motor-mouth seemed to be more in control. Not so impulsive. In fact, she was starting to feel as bright and pretty as some people said she was. What a nice dream, she thought. But wait 'til I wake up.

"You ever play football, Mr. B.?" Kram asked.

"Yes. High school and college. Do you play?"

"Sure," Kram said, happy that they had something in common. Maybe he'd look just like Mr. B. someday. Boy, he'd love to be that big. "What position do you play?" Kram asked.

"Noseguard."

"Hey! Me too," Kram said and stood a little taller.

"Oh Kram," Anna groaned, "now you think you're just like Mr. B."

How'd she read my mind? Kram wondered. Instead he said, "Ha! What do you know about football, anyway?"

"Oh, you two," Ms. Jensen said, shaking her head. "We'll all get a chance to know Mr. B. soon enough. He'll be helping each of you. But right now I'd like you to finish your journal writing. Remember I said we have a very big project coming up. I want to start it as soon as possible. It will be fun."

The kids settled down. They loved fun surprises. That's because most of their other surprises were terrible: big tests, and homework, and marks, and criticism. But what Ms. Jensen didn't know was that she was going to be the one who was the most surprised. By the kids. This was really going to be fun. For all of them. Especially Ms. Jensen.

6

Hello Hans

EVERYONE WONDERED what the new project would be. Even Mr. B.

With everyone staring at her, waiting, Ms. Jensen reached into her school bag and pulled out a poster that was rolled up.

Anna, never missing anything, watched. Then she quickly shouted, "Yes! Posters. We're going to get posters. Great project. I hope mine is a horse."

"No Anna. Just one poster. Door size. Or we could say, life size." Ms. Jensen unrolled the poster and taped it to the front wall, right next to the chalkboard. It was a picture of a man thinking. He was tall, thin, and had a twinkle in his eyes. He looked ready to play a joke or tell a funny story. Anna was sure he would be fun to know.

Ms. Jensen wrote a name on the board. HANS

HANS CHRISTIAN ANDERSEN

CHRISTIAN ANDERSEN. "Class, I'd like you to meet Hans Christian Andersen," she said, pointing to the poster.

"Hi Hans, how ya doin'," Funny-Freddie said, walking up to the poster to shake hands with it.

"I've heard that name before," Anna said, trying to remember where.

"Good try, Anna," Ms. Jensen responded. "I think many of you have heard of him before. What can you tell about him by looking at the poster?"

"He's tall and thin like me," Hyper-Harry said, jumping out of his seat. And by stretching, Harry tried to make himself look even taller and thinner. But he tripped over the leg of his chair, almost crashing to the floor. Embarrassed, he reached out like a wobbly drunk. "Hans. Help me. Help me." But something was wrong. Or different. He didn't fall this time. That was a first. Strange. What was happening to him?

The kids laughed. But they too wondered why Harry hadn't fallen. Somehow he didn't seem as klutzy as usual.

Ms. Jensen went over to Harry and jokingly offered to help him back to his seat. She knew he didn't need her help this time. And she even knew why. But she wasn't going to say anything to the class just yet. She just pretended he was the same as before.

"Harry," Ms. Jensen said, "in many ways Hans Christian Andersen is very much like you. Yes, you are both tall and thin. And some say he was awkward."

"What?" Bob-the-Fog said, as if he was waking up. "Awkward? What does that mean?" Although Bob said "What?" he didn't have to this time. He said it by habit—cause he always said it. Somehow the words he heard were clearer and slower sounding than ever before. And he seemed to understand what was said more quickly.

"It means clumsy or klutzy," Harry answered. "You see, I'm an awkward expert. I can teach anyone how to trip and fall and still survive."

Silently Harry thought, I hate the word "klutzy." But out loud he continued, "Yeah, Hans and Harry. We're a team. He's famous, right. Just like I'm gonna be someday. Is he a scientist? An astronaut? That's what I'm gonna be."

"He's not an astronaut," Kram said, figuring

things out. Somehow his mind was sharper and clearer. And his thinking-wheels were spinning smoothly and rapidly. He was now ready to score a mental touchdown.

"How do ya know that?" Anna asked.

"His clothes," Kram said. "They're old. Old-fashioned. He looks like he lived a hundred years ago. And there weren't any astronauts then."

"Excellent reasoning, Kram," Ms. Jensen said. "Amazing how you figured things out just by looking and then making intelligent decisions about it. Just like Sherlock Holmes, the famous detective. And I know what you're all thinking. No, Sherlock Holmes wasn't dyslexic. But he could have been." Then, returning to the poster, she said, "Hans Christian Andersen was born in 1805."

"Is he still alive?" Funny-Freddie asked with a slight grin.

"Dumb," Chuck grumbled. Perhaps he hadn't seen Freddie's grin and missed his joke. Perhaps he thought the teacher wouldn't hear him over everyone else's laughs. But Ms. Jensen heard. She knew what Chuck said wasn't nice. But she was at least glad Chuck was listening. Was he again trying to push everyone away with his nasty remarks? Or was he jealous of the other kids getting along with each other and herself? Maybe he's reaching out to them this time? Maybe he was trying to be part of the class this time? Although his remark wasn't nice, his voice didn't sound angry. Was this a clue that he was changing? Ms. Jensen sure hoped so.

Ignoring Chuck and kidding Freddie back, Ms. Jensen pretended to answer seriously, "No, Freddie. Hans is not alive. He died in 1875. Can anyone tell me how old he was when he died?"

Randy-the-Magician, who could never do math before, pulled out his calculator. Quickly he punched in 1875 take away 1805. "Seventy," Randy shouted, not able to hide his excitement. "Hans was seventy years old when he died." Strange, Randy thought to himself later on. I'm still able to remember the dates. Why didn't they erase? Am I losing my magic?

"Very good, Randy," Ms. Jensen smiled and wrote seventy years old on the board.

"Did he live in America?" Anna asked.

"No Anna, he lived in a very small country in

northern Europe called Denmark." Ms. Jensen then pulled down the world map and showed the class where Denmark was located.

"It's near Norway," Anna said. "That's where my Nanna came from. It must have been cold in Denmark because Nanna said it was very cold in Norway."

"Yes Anna," Ms. Jensen said, "Where Hans lived, to warm up, people liked to gather around fires and tell stories. And Hans was a great storyteller. The very, very best."

"I love to tell stories, too," Anna said.

"Yes Anna, I know you do. And just like you, Hans also had a problem writing them down. When people found his original papers, they were hard to read. Simple words were misspelled. Letters were backwards."

"Like mine," Kram said.

"And mine, too," Anna said, making a funny face at Kram. "What Hans needed was a computer."

"True, Anna," Ms. Jensen said, "but they didn't have computers back then."

"Then how could people read what he wrote?"

Anna asked. "If it weren't for the computer, no one could read what I wrote. Not even me."

"I'm sure he had someone to help him. Like a secretary. Someone to copy over his stories for him so others could read and enjoy them."

"A human computer," Funny-Freddie added. He sat up in his seat like a robot and tried to talk like one, too. "Yes sir, Mr. Hans. What story do I write today?" Then he wondered again to himself, Why didn't I fall? What's wrong? Something is different. I must be getting sick.

Everyone laughed at Freddie being a robot computer. Even Ms. Jensen. Even Mr. B. Chuck stared out the window...but one side of his mouth almost curled up in a smile. Just a little. Was he finally coming around?

"Were his parents rich so he could have a secretary?" Anna asked.

"Not at all, Anna. His father was a poor cobbler who made shoes. His mother could hardly read or write. And Hans was alone most of the time." Hearing that, Chuck looked up. He was like Hans, too. "Hans was a daydreamer, just like someone else we know," Ms. Jensen continued. Her remark caught

Bob's attention. And he didn't have to even ask, "What?" before understanding what she said. "Hans Christian Andersen had to struggle and work very hard to learn anything at all." Now all eyes were glued to the front of the room.

"H...he sounds l...like us," Amy's tiny voice whispered. Although Amy continued to hesitate with her words while speaking, she seemed to be speaking out more often. By herself, without being pushed to do so.

"Yes, Amy. That's smart of you to see that. Remember at the beginning of the year when we solved the mystery about why we have trouble learning?"

"Yeah, it's 'cause we have a disease," Freddie said, not laughing.

"Chicken pox," Hyper-Harry added, acting confused.

"NO!" Anna shouted, not realizing that Harry was just acting confused this time. "Not a disease. Not chicken pox. Dyslexia. It's like chicken pox cause some of us have lots of dyslexia and some of us only have a little."

"Anna, you remembered very well," Ms. Jensen

said. "Yes, dyslexia is when we see and write let-ters and words mixed up and backwards. Numbers, too. And some sounds are confused. Sometimes we feel awkward or clumsy."

"But wait," Hyper-Harry said. "If Hans had dyslexia like us, and he became famous, we could become famous, too."

"You're absolutely right," Ms. Jensen grinned. Even Ms. Jensen hadn't fully realized that Harry understood things better—and so he was joking more in class.

"I want to hear Hans' stories," Anna said.

"Good," Ms. Jensen smiled. "That's going to be part of our surprise project. We're going to hear four of Hans Christian Andersen's stories. But we're going to do it in a different way. It's going to include artwork."

"Yesss!" Magic-Randy, the artist, cheered.

"It's going to include writing."

"On the computer?" Anna asked. Ms. Jensen nodded, yes.

"Yesss!" Anna cheered.

"It will include acting."

"Yesss!" Funny-Freddie cheered, standing up and

bowing. Anna was good at that, too. Maybe she'd help him? And she was pretty, too. That wouldn't be so bad, either, Freddie thought. She'll be my leading lady.

"It will include math," Ms. Jensen continued. "We are going to make a huge mural. That's a large picture. So we'll have to figure out how much space to give each story and each person."

"I can do that on my calculator," Hyper-Harry said.

"I can dream up ideas," Bob-the-Fog said, rapidly coming out of his fog. Everybody giggled.

"Yes, Bob," Ms. Jensen responded. "I'm sure your daydreams will help make this project fun. Imaginations can be very exciting."

"Can we get sports in it? Football?" Kram asked.

"I'm sure you'll figure out a way to get football into the project," Ms. Jensen said.

"How about horses? Can it be about horses?" Anna asked.

"M...music?" Amy asked, once again responding without needing any encouragement.

"I'm sure there will be something in it for *everyone.*" Chuck looked up. He didn't like the sound of that. His dark eyes froze on Ms. Jensen. *Not me*, those eyes said. But this time Ms. Jensen didn't look away. Her stare met Chuck's. And she didn't blink, either. Yes, her eyes said. This time, you will be part of the class. Defiantly, Chuck shoved his arms across his chest. He locked both hands to his sides. No, his eyes said. But Ms. Jensen smiled. She looked like she had a secret. A plan. Slowly she turned to the rest of the class. "Tomorrow we will begin Hans Christian Andersen's first story, 'The Ugly Duckling.' I will read it," she said, holding up a small book full of his stories.

"But there are no pictures," Randy-the-Magician said, disappointed.

"No," Ms. Jensen said. "The pictures will be the ones that you see in your head. The pictures that Hans creates for you with his words. And tomorrow I will divide this class into four groups. How many will be in each group?" Ms. Jensen asked.

"Two kids per group," Kram said. He was always good at math. Didn't even need a calculator. But he liked using one anyway. Just to make sure. And for the fun of it.

"Right, Kram. For the next few weeks you all will be working in two's."

Chuck's killer look hit the teacher.

"Who's with who?" Hyper-Harry asked nervously. If she puts me with Chuck, he thought, I'm dead.

"Who's with whom," Ms. Jensen corrected automatically. "And you will have to wait to find that out," she smiled. "Now please line up. It's time for gym."

They loved gym lately. It was fun. They had been doing crazy things with a parachute. No balls to catch and throw. But as they lined up at the door, they kept looking at each other and wondering. Are you my partner? You? Or you? Anna looked at Kram thinking, I could take Kram as my partner. He's cute even if we do fight all the time. Even if he isn't as strong and handsome as Mr. B.

Chuck stayed back in his seat. He looked like he wanted to melt. He was steaming hot. His arms stayed crossed. Those killer eyes darted around the room. No way, his eyes said. Not me. No partner. Alone. I'm a loner.

But Ms. Jensen smiled and softly called out,

"Come on, Chuck. Gym." There was something about Ms. Jensen's voice that scared him. She seemed confident. In control. More so than before. And he felt the opposite. Less in control. Like he was being forced to listen. Worse. *Like we wanted to listen!* Chuck stood up, then he kicked his chair. *CRASH!* It fell over. He was trying to put up his same old fight. But there was no real fight left in him. He was just acting. Trying to fool himself. And the rest of the class, too.

Freddie-the-Clown shivered, thinking, Oh boy. I hope Chuck's not my partner. Freddie looked around. Who would get Chuck? Who would want him? Who?

7

Partners

THE NEXT DAY, around mid-morning, Ms. Jensen gathered the eight Upside-Down Kids around her on her "talking rug." She held the book of short stories by Hans Christian Andersen on her lap.

Because the kids had trouble reading, they all loved it when a story was read out loud. And Ms. Jensen was a great reader and story-teller. She made the characters come alive. To encourage their interest in books, she read to the class almost every day. So far this year their favorites were *The Velveteen Rabbit*, *Charlotte's Web*, *Winnie-The-Pooh*, and *The Wind in the Willows*. They liked animal stories the best.

But as they sat quietly, ready to listen, they knew that this story would be different. They were going to be separated into groups of two after the story. And they were going to have to do something special with the story. But they didn't know what. So they listened extra hard. Bob-the-Fog sat right up front. This kept his mind from daydreaming. Chuck stayed in the back. This kept him apart from the class. But Ms. Jensen knew he always listened to her stories anyway. Even from the back. Even when he looked out the window. She really hoped that this new project, and the partner she chose for Chuck, would help him become part of the class. She knew it would force him to make a decision. And she felt he was now ready to choose her and the class over running away. But she couldn't be sure. She prayed his decision would be the right one. She didn't want to lose him. Not now. Not after all the effort they spent getting this far.

Ms. Jensen then said to the class, "The first story I'm going to read by Hans Christian Andersen is called 'The Ugly Duckling.' It's really very good. So I'm sure you're going to like it. But you all will have to listen very carefully. Because after the story I'm going to see just how many things you all can remember about it."

Ms. Jensen looked at Motor-Mouth-Anna and

then Bob-the-Fog. She said, "Anna. Bob. You two will be the first group. This will become your story. I want you to pay special attention."

Bob-the-Fog looked around. He was glad now that he was sitting up front. Staring at Ms. Jensen's face and reading her lips made it easier for him to hear clearly. He was glad Anna was his partner. Because she understood things quickly, not like him, and talked so easily. She'll do most of the work, he thought. Bob relaxed. Once again he realized that he didn't need to say "What?" before understanding conversations. But he didn't say anything, fearing it would soon disappear.

Anna looked around. No Kram to work with. Too bad. Oh well, she decided, we'd probably just fight all the time anyway. Better with Bob. He won't argue. He'll go along with what I say. But I hope he'll listen. Not just daydream. Oops, Anna suddenly realized that Ms. Jensen had started reading. I'd better stop daydreaming and listen, she thought.

The kids were quiet during the story Ms. Jensen read. They listened. They laughed. They felt sad. They felt happy. When Ms. Jensen finished reading she asked, "Who can tell me what happened first?"

"It was summer," Anna said, always the first to talk. But, she thought, this was her story anyway.

"There was a turkey," Funny-Freddie said.

"No Freddie, not a turkey," Kram responded. "There was a big egg in the duck's nest so they thought it was a turkey egg."

"Yeah, but when it hatched it was bigger than the other ducklings. So they thought it was a turkey-duck," Randy laughed.

"And they were really mean to the ugly duckling," Anna added. "They bit him. Chickens pecked at him. He was shoved around."

Bob added. "He was really sad 'cause he was laughed at and chased away by everyone. Even his own brother and sister rejected him. So he ran away." Bob-the-Fog looked like he really understood what the ugly duckling felt. All too often, Bob had thought about running away from his brother, Tim.

"But when the duckling ran away," Hyper-Harry said, "he thought he'd be like the geese. They were bigger. But then he saw them being shot by a hunter. So he decided not to be a goose. Smart duck," Harry added.

Everyone laughed.

"H...he was alone and cold all winter," Amy said. Just like me, Chuck thought. Ms. Jensen could hear that Amy's speaking was getting better. So could the rest of the class. But Amy was afraid to face up to her improvement. Afraid it would disappear. Good things never lasted for those kids. Except for Ms. Jensen. She was the best thing that ever happened to them.

"Ta da! Spring came," Anna added.

"And the ugly duck saw three beautiful swans on the lake. I could draw them," Randy-the-Magician said. Strange. He remembered most of the story.

"But it was the best when the ugly duckling saw his own reflection and realized he was a *beautiful* swan," Anna chimed in. Then she began to quote from the story. "He was 'happy, but not proud, because a good heart is never proud.' "

"Very good, Anna," Ms. Jensen said. "You even remembered Mr. Andersen's own words. And you all did an excellent job telling me what happened in the beginning, in the middle and in the end. Good listeners. Now who can tell me why the duckling felt different?"

"'Cause he was bigger than the others," Kram-the-Ram said.

"And he was klutzy," Hyper-Harry said.

"Everyone picked on him," Bob-the-Fog added.

"Everyone pecked on him," Funny-Freddy joked.

"So what did the ugly duckling do?" Ms. Jensen asked.

"He ran away," Randy-the-Magician said.

"Did that help?" Ms. Jensen asked.

"No," Anna responded. "He still felt ugly. But he didn't give up. Then he saw his reflection in the water. And he saw he wasn't ugly anymore."

"He was h...happy," Silent-Amy smiled. She liked this story. Maybe someday she wouldn't stutter anymore. Maybe she wouldn't feel like an ugly duckling herself. She decided never to give up trying. One day she might be able to talk like Anna. Then she smiled to herself and thought, No one can talk like Anna. Almost like Anna?

Ms. Jensen responded, "Yes, the ugly duckling was finally happy with himself. Anna and Bob, this is your story. In a few weeks you will have worked out you own special way to present it to the class. You may write a report, a poem, another story, a song, a play...anything you want. And you will illustrate it on the paper in the hall. Harry, would you please go out with your calculator and divide the mural into five equal sections?"

"Five?" Anna questioned, "I thought there would be just four groups."

"Right," Ms. Jensen said, "but Randy, I would like you to go out and do the first section all by yourself. First draw the title, TALES BY HANS CHRISTIAN ANDERSEN. And with your great artistic ability, do you think you could draw this picture of Hans from my book?" Ms. Jensen asked, holding out her book for Randy to see.

Magic-Randy looked at the picture. "Sure. I could draw that. His hair's pretty long. Curly. A little bald on top. Kinda big nose. Nice eyes. Nice smile. A bow tie. Sure, I could draw him. Can I start now?" For some reason, he seemed very sure of himself. Confident! Just the opposite of the way he usually felt.

Ms. Jensen liked his enthusiasm. "Yes. You and Harry can go out now and measure. You may begin penciling in what you want. Anna and Bob, why don't you go in the corner and begin brainstorming. See what ideas you come up with. And jot them down. The rest of you may pick out some games to play."

Kram grabbed the *Yahtzee*. He liked number games better than letter games like *Scrabble*. But he had to admit he was usually pretty good at guessing the words in hangman. Funny-Freddie and Silent-Amy joined him for the game. Chuck grabbed the tape recorder. Ms. Jensen had lots of stories on tape for the class to listen to. Chuck pulled out *Treasure Island*. Then he flipped the tape on in the recorder and put on the earphones. And as he stared out the window into the cold snow, his mind traveled thousands of miles away to a warm tropical island. He was using the tape to escape from the class rather than to learn reading. Escape was now more important than learning to read.

Before the story began, Chuck noticed that the old oak leaf was still hanging on the tree. Even in the freezing snow. Like magic. It hung in there. Just like the ugly duckling. Just like he did. Hangin' on, even when he wanted to give up. Run away. And forget it all. But he knew his mom needed him. And he felt Ms. Jensen and the class wanted him—

despite how bad he acted. Suddenly, he realized that maybe his mom was just hangin' on, too. That scared him. What would happen if she let go? What would happen if Ms. Jensen let go? What would happen if he let go? He didn't want to think about it all. Back to the *Treasure Island* tape. Escape.

8

Soldiers and Emperors

LATER ON THAT WEEK, Ms. Jensen once again gathered her class around her on the "talking rug." This time Mr. B. read Hans Christian Andersen's story, "The Steadfast Tin Soldier."

Kram liked Mr. B. He talked with him a lot about football. Kram also liked how he read, too. Mr. B. could really make his voice low. Or loud. He made the story fun. Alive. Real.

After the story, Mr. B. asked, "What happened first in the story?"

Hyper-Harry responded first, even before Anna, "The tin soldier was born in a box with twenty-five others. Then they all jumped out of the box except for one soldier. That soldier couldn't cause he had only one leg. And he had only one leg cause the guy who made him ran out of tin. Maybe when God made me, he ran out of computer chips. Maybe that's why I'm so stupid and klutzy." Harry started walking around like a stiff robot gone wild. He pretended to knock into desks and chairs. Everyone laughed. Everyone except Harry. He was too busy thinking about his improved balance and coordination.

Mr. B. understood Harry's joke about himself. He could see that Harry was thinking about his dyslexic symptoms and how they were related to the story characters. Dr. L.'s therapy must be working well for Hyper-Harry. He seemed calmer. His thinking was clearer. And despite his joking, he seemed less klutzy and less disorganized. Then Mr. B. asked, "So there was one tin soldier in the box that had only one leg. He was different from the others. What happened next?"

The s...soldier loved the ballerina," Amy said.

"Yeah," Anna added, "he loved her cause he thought she had one leg just like him. But her other leg was just hiding under her skirt."

"Then all sorts of things happened to the soldier,"

Hyper-Harry added, "after he fell out of the box."

"Two kids put him in a paper boat and sailed him down a river," Magic-Randy said. But then he thought to himself: Did I remember that or did I just make it up? He couldn't believe his memory was improving.

"He passed a giant rat," Bob-the-Fog rapidly chimed in, "and then he was eaten by a fish. Definitely a bad day." But Bob was having better days. He was definitely hearing things clearer and understanding them more rapidly.

Kram-the-Football-Ram added, "And then the soldier ended up in the same house where he started from. The maid cut open the fish and found him."

"Then she threw him in the fire. Nice ending," Chuck said sarcastically. But at least he participated. And he didn't feel as angry as before. As angry as he sounded.

"B...but the ballerina was knocked in, too," Amy said. "That's sad. That's romantic."

"Did the soldier ever give up?" Mr. B. asked.

"Never," Hyper-Harry said, standing at attention without falling, his hand over his heart. "He stood steadfast."

"And when he melted, he turned into a tin heart," Anna added. "He was a good guy."

"Lotta good it did him," Chuck sneered. Shut up, Chuck said to himself. Why am I going along with this stupid project? And he didn't like the next thought that occurred to him: Because I want to.

Mr. B. overlooked Chuck's remark. He looked at Kram. "Kram and Harry, this is your story. You two can go in the back and begin brainstorming about your picture for the mural and what you want to present to the class. Anna and Bob, you may continue your work on 'The Ugly Duckling.' The rest of you have game time."

Magic-Randy, Funny-Freddie and Silent-Amy went to the chalkboard for a game of hangman. Chuck checked out the tapes again and decided on Jack London's *Call of the Wild.* There were many, many tapes to choose from. Because every time Ms. Jensen read a story to the class, she recorded what she read. The class library of *talking books* was really growing.

Ms. Jensen found these tapes to be extremely helpful for kids who found reading difficult. This

way dyslexics could learn by listening. And it was even possible to listen to a story while attempting to read. That way you heard the words you saw. And you didn't have to keep looking them up in a dictionary you couldn't understand anyway. Also, the better you understood the story, the easier it was to figure out the words you were looking at.

On the next Monday, the kids sat waiting to hear Hans Christian Andersen's third story. They waited for the verdict: Who was going to get stuck with Killer-Chuck?

Ms. Jensen began, "Today's story is *'The Emporer's New Clothes.'* "

"Oh no," Anna said, turning red and giggling. "I've heard this one before." Anna was very glad she already had her story. She wouldn't want to act this story out before the rest of the class!

"Ssssh," Freddie frowned. He wanted to hear the story. 'Cause he had a feeling it would be his.

Ms. Jensen began reading. The story was really funny. All the kids laughed a lot. Even Chuck smiled. But then covered his mouth like Amy used to so no one could see. Sometimes their faces turned red out of embarrassment. It was a different kind of story for school. About being naked and stuff like that.

After she finished reading, Ms. Jensen asked, "What was the story about?"

"A guy who ran around with no clothes on," Magic-Randy said, rolling over laughing. Once again he thought to himself, How come I remembered? What's happening to my computer chips?

But Anna was serious and added, "That was just 'cause the tailors said if you couldn't see the new clothes, you were stupid. So no one wanted to say they couldn't see the clothes. No one wanted to be called stupid. So they all stupidly made believe they saw his clothes."

Ms. Jensen asked, "Was it true that if you couldn't see the Emperor's clothes you were stupid?"

"No," Kram said, "you were stupid if you said you saw them and you didn't."

"What are some of the things that people call *you* stupid for?" Ms. Jensen asked.

"If you spell words wrong," Funny-Freddie grumbled.

"And mess up the times tables, or knock over real

tables when you walk," Hyper-Harry and Magic-Randy said, almost together.

"When you can't hear too well and then ask '*what?*' all the time," Bob-the-Fog said.

"When you read out loud and make dumb mistakes on simple words. Then you feel stupid," Kram-the-Ram added. But he had stopped making so many reading mistakes. Strange.

"When you keep forgetting things like names, lists, dates, even days and telling time," Magic-Randy answered again, almost in a whisper. But he wasn't forgetting all these things lately.

"When you talk funny," Silent-Amy whispered. But this time without stuttering or mumbling.

"Or when your writing is so bad," Anna said, "that people call me...oops, ya, stupid." But her writing was getting better. Even without the computer.

"Nobody calls me stupid," Chuck-the-Terror growled. "Nobody." But he wasn't as angry as he sounded. And he didn't even scare the other kids so much anymore, either.

"Are you really stupid if you can't do those things?" Ms. Jensen continued.

"No!" Kram said suddenly seeing the light. "Like the Emperor was the one who was really stupid by pretending he still saw the clothes. Like people or kids are really stupid when they call others stupid. Maybe it's 'cause they're afraid of the stupid in themselves."

"Wow Kram," Ms. Jensen smiled. "You surprise me. That was very good. Maybe you should be a psychiatrist when you grow up."

"Sure," Kram-the-Ram said, blushing. Ms. Jensen's compliment sure made him feel good inside. "Maybe after I play pro football," Kram answered while smiling at Mr. B.

After the kids voiced their opinions and settled down, Ms. Jensen continued, "Randy and Freddie, this is your story."

Both Randy and Freddie sighed with relief. They didn't get Killer-Chuck. "Great!" Magic-Randy shouted, jumping up. "I'll draw the picture. Freddie, you get to be the Emperor. So when you trip and fall, you won't tear your clothes. Ha, ha, ha. You won't be wearing anything to rip."

"Okay," Funny-Freddie laughed, always ready to be the clown. He started unbuttoning his shirt.

"Nooo!" Anna screamed. Everyone giggled and laughed as Funny-Freddie danced around clowning, half taking off his shirt.

Ms. Jensen finally regained the kids' attention again. They were all excited. Really high. "You're doing great. We only have one last story. So we'll begin with it tomorrow."

Suddenly Anna looked around the room. And for the first time, she thought rather than spoke. Anna knew the last group had to be Amy and Chuck. Poor Amy. She's going to be murdered. Anna shivered. Glad I'm not Amy.

But, Anna noticed, Amy seemed calm and remained quiet. She must know something we don't. Maybe she doesn't mind dying or something like that? Or maybe she's just plain crazy and we never knew it.

And Chuck. He just stared out the window at that old dumb leaf. The sky was dark. Filled with huge heavy white clouds.

More snow? Anna wondered while looking out of Chuck's window. She hoped so for Amy's sake, but not for hers. She and Bob were making up the best story ever. She couldn't wait to finish it and get it

105

on the computer. The kids would love it. She was
sure of it. They would really love it. But what about
poor Amy? she wondered. What's going to happen
to her?

9

The Prince and the Princess

THE NEXT MORNING the kids woke up to a snow blizzard. Overnight, eight inches had fallen and it was still coming down heavy. The snow was so thick that you could hardly see your own hands in front of your face. Icy winds howled around corners and whipped down the middle of the empty streets. Only emergency cars were allowed on the roads. Everyone was told to stay home. Schools were closed.

Anna thought about Amy when she turned over in bed to grab a little more sleep. The snow saved her. Amy had one more day before she had to work with Killer-Chuck. This was a lucky day for Amy.

But Chuck was really upset when he saw all the snow. His house was freezing. To warm things up, he had to put pots of boiling water on the stove. And when his mom finally fell asleep, he went out. Ducking his head against the freezing wind and snow, he walked and walked. He didn't know where he was going. And he didn't care. Snow collected on his hair turning it white and frozen. Ice flakes stuck to his eyelashes and eyebrows, turning them white. Chilled, he pulled his collar up. School was bad, Chuck thought, but staying home was worse. While walking, he kicked snow. And pushed his frozen gloveless hands deep down within his jeans pockets. He felt cold. Inside and out. Alone. Worried. Amy wasn't like the others. He couldn't bully her or be mean to her. She was always nice. He knew she was very, very sensitive. And in pain. Like his mom...but different. But whether the pain was felt in the body, or caused by worry, it still hurt. And it hurt just as bad. That he knew. He couldn't upset Amy by not showing up or pushing her away with meanness. What could he do? What would he do?

The blizzard raged for two days. And so did Chuck. The kids didn't have to go back to school until the next week. And so Chuck sulked and sulked. He was trapped and didn't know what to do. All the running on the track had stopped in January. Too much snow. And February was freezing and snowy, too. Somehow the running made Chuck feel better. It cleared his mind and his concentration, too. Even his frustrations and anxieties were at an all-time low. Running was like a tranquilizer for him. And so was Ms. Jensen. For the first time in a long, long time he felt someone really cared about him. Really, really cared. How could he disappoint her? How could he hurt her?

Monday, when they were finally back in class, Ms. Jensen said, "I think that was winter's last hurrah! It's the end of February. And hopefully that will be the last of the snow. I don't know about you kids, but I'm ready for Spring and running again." They nodded in agreement. Even Chuck felt himself silently saying, Yes. He didn't feel comfortable with his growing attachment to Ms. Jensen. But it didn't make him as angry or scared as before. Not as crazy and wild. In fact, he sort of liked it.

Freddie said, "Spring's okay, but I *love* snow days!"

"Yesss!" the class cheered.

"Okay," Ms. Jensen grinned. "I think there's

been too much vacation for you guys. Right after today's journal writing, we'll read Hans Christian Andersen's last tale. You do remember who Hans Christian Andersen is, don't you?"

They all laughed. Even Chuck thought it was funny. And the joke was on him. How could he forget who Hans was? Hans was the guy that was turning him inside out and upside down.

The kids liked it when Ms. Jensen joked. Her kidding made them all feel like one. Like working harder. Like wanting to succeed. They copied the journal question, IF YOU LIVED AT THE NORTH POLE, HOW WOULD YOUR LIFE BE DIFFERENT? A fun question. And besides, they were really good at this journal writing by now. Sometimes those five minutes of writing went by so fast they even begged Ms. Jensen to give them more time. They loved not having to worry about spelling or grammar or penmanship. All the things that made them feel stupid. That made them hate writing out their thoughts and feelings. Ms. Jensen let them bypass their problems. And so they had fun trying to be creative.

At the end of each week, Ms. Jensen encouraged the kids to share one journal entry with the rest

D-G-O
=
DOG

H-T-A
=
HAT

C-T-A
=
CAT

of the class, if they wanted to. So they tried to make it good. Perfect. They even corrected the spelling. But it was no big deal. Ms. Jensen never used a red pen. In fact, she threw them all out. Using a regular light pencil, she just circled the misspelled words. Then they could use a dictionary to find the answer. And they could erase her pencil marks. But most of the kids liked to use SR. And everyone kept a list of words that gave them the most trouble. They were learning to write and spell and think. But for the first time learning was enjoyable. They learned because they wanted to. Not because they were forced to. And for some reason they all found learning easier than ever before. Silently they all wondered if it had anything to do with Dr. L. and his treatment.

"Okay," Ms. Jensen said. "Pencils down." She then asked the kids to gather around on the "talking rug." The magic rug enabled them to feel closer to one another. And to concentrate and listen better.

Mr. B. opened the book. Everyone knew this was Amy and Chuck's story, but no one said anything. Mr. B. began reading "The Princess and the Pea."

Quiet filled the room. Only Mr. B.'s deep voice

filled it with action. When he finished, Mr. B. asked, "How did this story begin?"

Foggy-Bob liked the story because he heard it clearly. Easily. Without distraction. And without confusion as before. So he started talking, "You see there was this Prince. And he wanted a Princess." Bob's eyes widened as he looked around the room, like he was saying, yeah, what a great idea.

"But it had to be a *real* Princess," Magic-Randy said, remembering more than he ever did before.

"Then one dark stormy night, in a thunder and lightning storm," Funny-Freddie said shivering. He hated thunder and lightning. But it didn't sound as loud as before. And it didn't scare him as much. Am I going deaf, he wondered. Or am I braver? Little did he know that he was getting better.

Anna continued for Funny-Freddie, "A girl came to the castle. She was wet and ugly-looking from the storm, but she was a *real* princess."

"So the old Queen decided to put her to the test," Kram-the-Ram said. "And she slipped a pea under her mattresses...to see if she was real."

"Under twenty mattresses!" Harry said. "I could sleep on twenty mattresses."

"But she couldn't sleep," Amy said without stuttering.

"Yeah, 'cause she was a real princess and the pea was a pain in the...back," Anna giggled.

"Right," Mr. B. added. "Some people are very sensitive. Just like the Princess. Just like you kids. Some people are very sensitive to touch or pain. Even sound and motion sensitive. And some people get their feelings hurt very easily. And there are those who are sensitive to lights. Especially flourescent lights."

Upon hearing and understanding Mr. B.'s last remark, Bob-the-Fog pushed his tinted glasses up on his nose. And then he tilted his baseball cap up to show the class his magic hat. He wore it all over— when he could. Just like the sunglasses, it shielded his eyes from the light. That helped him read and concentrate better. And so he didn't have to ask "What?" so often. In fact, he knew exactly what Mr. B. was talking about.

Mr. B. added, "Some people are sensitive to things they eat or breathe and have allergies."

"*Aaachooo!*" Funny-Freddie faked a funny sneeze.

"Some people are even very sensitive to how they

speak, read, write, or walk," Mr. B. continued. Now all the kids looked at one another and started to squirm. "Some are sensitive about things that happen in their home. With their families." As Chuck looked down, Mr. B. stood up. He towered over them all. His voice grew louder and stronger as he said, "Being sensitive is *not* bad. Everyone is sensitive in one way or another. Being sensitive makes you a very special person."

"Like a Princess?" Amy said, smiling. She realized that for once she said something without stuttering at all. But her stuttering had stopped before, too, without her knowing it.

"Or a Prince," Foggy-Bob said, standing tall while again pushing his sunglasses up on his nose. He walked around with his baseball cap on his head as if he were wearing a King's crown.

Ms. Jensen once again joined the group. "Chuck and Amy, now you have your story to tell. You may begin right away. The rest of you can work on your own projects. I know some of you are in the middle of drawing pictures on the mural. And some are writing. So I can hardly wait to see what wonderful ideas you come up with. It's all very exciting. And

I'm amazed that you've been able to keep everything secret from the rest of the kids."

The class scattered. Some read. Some cut. Some pasted. Some wrote or typed at the computer. Some went into the hall to add to the mural. Amy and Chuck walked over to the table in the back of the room and sat down. They remained quiet for a long time. Ms. Jensen held her breath and prayed for Chuck and Amy to begin. Finally, she saw Chuck say something. And Amy nodded back. Ms. Jensen took another deep breath and sighed with relief. She began to feel that Chuck and Amy *would* help each other. They *would* survive. And she hoped that Chuck would hang in there long enough to make it.

10

Perfect Projects

WEEKS PASSED. The mural in the hall was almost completed. Randy, the artist, always had an extra finishing touch to add here or there. The mural became the pride of the school. Kids came over from all the other classes to ask about Hans Christian Andersen. To ask about the four stories. To admire the pictures. Everyone was talking about what a great mural it was. And the Upside-Down Kids were happy to answer questions and explain the drawings. They felt good about what they had done. And they were now considered experts on Hans. For the very first time ever in school, they were treated with respect by the other kids. Usually, the Upside-Down Kids were looked down on. And considered dumb or crazy. Weird. Not this time!

Now it was finally time for the group presentation. A nervous excitement ran through the class. Anna couldn't sit still. "Us first, us first," she called out. "You're gonna love it. Love it. What a story," Anna jumped up. "Remember, our story was 'The Ugly Duckling.' "

Anna had been amazed at Foggy-Bob's great ideas. He had always seemed to be in a fog. Yet now he was great. And his fog appeared to be clearing up. That made things easier. As a result, they really worked well as a team. They wrote their story together, often using SR. Then they entered it into the computer and printed it out. They even divided up their story so that they both took turns speaking and listening. Anna controlled her impulsive speaking and even enjoyed hearing what Foggy-Bob had to say. And Bob was learning to hear and understand things clearly and rapidly. Ms. Jensen nodded for them to begin. Foggy-Bob joined Anna in front of the class. He wore his tinted glasses and his baseball cap. Magically, they made it easier for him to read his part. The letters and words seemed clearer. And they didn't jump around and twist so much. He felt nervous. But not sick or dizzy. And not as nervous as before. Anna's palms were sweaty holding the paper. But she was glad it would be easier to read the neatly typed words. The printer enlarged the words and spelling so that they were easier to see and follow. I know what Dr. L. would say, she thought. It's easier for my missile-eyes to hit a big, fat, dark letter and word than small, thin, light ones. Anna and Bob started their story.

BOB:

A Story About the Planet Izi

It was beautiful in outer space. The rocket ship whizzed past the moon. And the stars. Into other galaxies, leaving their home planet behind. Suddenly, the rocket ship started to shake violently.

ANNA:

"Aba! Aba! What is happening?" Eve screamed.

BOB:

"We're being sucked into a black hole. Buckle up, Eve. Hold on tight. We'll make..." But Aba's voice was lost. The pressure on his chest became too heavy for him to speak.

ANNA:

Aba and Eve passed out. Their ship moved faster and faster. Faster through time. Faster through eternity. Faster through the forever black hole. *CRASH!* Everything stopped.

BOB:

Aba and Eve shook their heads trying to clear them. "We're not moving anymore," Aba said. He looked out the little window. Eve opened the door. Slowly they walked down the steps of their ship.

ANNA:

"Weird," Eve said, looking around. "The sky is yellow. The ground is purple. The trees have brown tops. But the tops are on the ground. And the green trunks and roots reach up high into the yellow sky. Crazy. Everything is upside down and backwards."

BOB:

"Ssssh. Someone or something is coming," Aba said. Funny giant people walked backwards to Aba and Eve. They waved go away. But when Aba and Eve started to move back, the giants loudly grumbled and jumbled until Aba and Eve followed them. They meant for them to go forward.

ANNA:

"They do everything backwards," Eve whispered to Aba. She and Aba tried to walk backwards, too. But they kept stumbling and falling.

BOB:

The giants had only one eye in the middle of their red bald heads. And many points grew out, resembling a crown. The giants laughed at Aba and Eve's clumsy attempts to walk backwards. The giants were sure that two eyes made it difficult to move without tripping and falling. One eye was better than two. The giants laughed loud and hard at the funny-looking creatures that landed on their planet. Even the trees shook from their laughter. And as the green trunks waved in the yellow sky, they also appeared to be laughing at the funny couple.

ANNA:

Tripping, again, Eve complained, "Aba, they are laughing at us." She said that in a soft voice. The giants thought her low voice was funny, too. So they all started whispering to each other. They thought whispering was so funny it made them fall down laughing. They rolled all over the purple grass.

BOB:

Aba and Eve felt ugly and stupid and clumsy. They tried to do things like the giants. But they couldn't.

After becoming friends, Eve showed the giants how to draw pictures in the black sand using their fingers. They liked that and thought she must be very clever. Aba took their picture with a Polaroid camera. They were shocked and excited to see themselves. And when they laughed and danced around Aba and Eve, the ground shook. Eve thought it was an earthquake. Or maybe she should say an Iziquake.

ANNA:

The giants helped Aba and Eve fix their spaceship. They kept yelling, "abA! evE! emoC kcaB oT izI. emoC kcaB oT iZI.

BOB:

> On the trip back to earth they tried to figure out the giants' message. Suddenly Aba said, "They got our names right. And I could tell that the last word was their planet."

ANNA:

> Then Eve shouted, "I've got it. Aba. Eve. COME BACK TO IZI. That's it. They spoke backwards. But our names and their planet's name are the same backwards and forwards. Aba and Eve smiled. They knew they met people who were different. But they could still be friends with them. And they could all learn from each other.
>
> The end.

Dead silence filled the room. Suddenly Freddie-the-Clown jumped up shouting, "Bravo. Bravo," because he heard that's what you're supposed to call out if you like a play. He clapped his hands as loud as he could. The other kids stood and clapped, too. So did Ms. Jensen and Mr. B. Anna and Foggy-Bob felt great. They had worked hard on their story. And they were glad that everyone else liked it.

Ms. Jensen walked to the front of the room. "I'm so proud of you both. I'm sure Hans Christian Andersen would be proud of you, too. You wrote a modern day fairy tale. And we all loved it."

"I think that deserves a party," Mr. B. said. And Ms. Jensen agreed. So Mr. B. went to the little refrigerator in the back of the room and took out cheese, crackers, peanut butter, and orange juice. Everyone ate—even Chuck. Then Hyper-Harry said to Anna and Foggy-Bob, "I really liked how you made Aba and Eve's name the same frontwards and backwards. That was clever."

Anna and Bob smiled at each other. Then Anna said, "Kinda like, Bob and Anna, isn't it?"

"Wow," said Hyper-Harry. "I never thought of that before. Anna and Bob can be reversed. They are the same forward and backward." Harry thought for a minute. "Yrrah. Nope. Guess it doesn't work with Harry," he laughed.

After the party, everyone settled down again. They were ready for the next presentation. What a great day.

Ms. Jensen then announced, "Kram and Harry, you're next."

Hyper-Harry calmly bounced his way to the front of the room. He was getting better. Dr. L.'s medicine was helping. He didn't feel like his inner motor was racing so fast. And his concentration and reading were better, too. But best of all, he didn't stumble so much. But he could still be clumsy. Especially when he was nervous. And he was nervous now.

Kram didn't smile. His stomach was in knots. He hated to read. And reading in front of the class was the worst. But he'd try. And so he tried real hard and finally got Harry to read the story for him. But if for some reason Harry couldn't read it, Kram had memorized what they were going to say. Sweat formed on his brow. He was sure glad Anna wasn't his partner. He would have never been able to memorize the long story she and Bob wrote, but as he memorized the story, he felt something strange within him. The words he read looked clear and easy to see. They were no longer moving on the page. And his eyes no longer lost their place while he read. And they didn't get stuck on the letters and words anymore, either. His "reading stutter" had somehow magically disappeared.

Kram started talking. He was better at talking than reading. "Uh, hi. Okay, we're ready," he looked at Harry. Harry was standing next to him bouncing up and down on the balls of his feet. Not because his motor raced. But because he was anxious. And moving calmed him down. "Okay. Our story was 'The Steadfast Tin Soldier.' You remember it?" he asked, looking around at everyone. The kids nodded, yes.

"Okay. Well, we checked around 'cause I remembered reading about this kid playing football. With one leg. In high school, see. So anyway, that must have been pretty hard. 'Cause I know football's hard. So anyway, he must have been pretty tough. You know, steadfast. Our story isn't very long." Kram gave a worried glance at Ms. Jensen. She nodded that was fine. "Okay. Here," Kram said, passing the paper to Harry.

Hyper-Harry stood still. Like a statue. No one had ever seen him stand so still before. They listened.

"There was once a boy in high school.
Who the kids all thought was real cool.
He played on the team.

A tackle so mean.

With one leg he really did rule."

"Yesss!" Funny-Freddie cheered, standing and clapping. Everyone joined him.

"Great," Anna added.

"There's a baseball player with one arm in the pros," Chuck said.

The class and Ms. Jensen were amazed. Delighted. Chuck had never before cooperated in a class event. He just couldn't. But now he could and did. And he was not angry or too anxious. Just shocked at his own participation. Ms. Jensen warmly and approvingly nodded to him. Then deliberately skipping over Chuck, Ms. Jensen asked, "Is that really true, Kram?"

"Yup," Kram said, "I read it in the paper. And also about the baseball player with one arm that Chuck mentioned. Well, I didn't really read about it...I overheard someone else reading it."

"Well I am impressed," Ms. Jensen said. "I also liked how you and Chuck connected the players to the steadfast tin soldier. They're good examples of people who never gave up. Who don't quit, no matter what. Just like the soldier. Just like you all. Everyone has problems. And some are worse than others. Yet it's always amazing to see those who are steadfast and determined. They're capable of super things. Like the football player with one leg or the baseball player with one arm. Like all you Upside-Down Kids. When you want something enough, and work really hard, it is amazing what can be accomplished. What an excellent morning this has been. We'll break for lunch now," Ms. Jensen continued. "And when we return, we'll hear what Randy and Freddie have prepared for us."

Funny-Freddie jumped up. "You're gonna love it. You're gonna love it. It's funny. I'm not telling why." But Freddie couldn't hold back completely. "I'll give you a clue," he grinned. "It's called *Stupid*. You're gonna love it." Freddie laughed as he skipped down the hall. Freddie felt good. Once again, he and the rest of the Upside-Down Kids didn't feel so upside down anymore. They raced to lunch. And for the first time, Chuck did not remain behind. Alone.

After filling up on hamburgers and fries, the kids were eager to get back into the classroom and hear about *Stupid*. No one spoke about it, but they were a little nervous to hear what Chuck and Amy were going to do. They couldn't really believe Chuck would cooperate with Amy. But they would wait and see. And hope. Randy was too excited to eat lunch, which was very unusual. He felt like his stomach was already full...of butterflies. Suddenly, *CRACK!* A loud smack filled the room. Funny-Freddie had slammed a book down on a desk to get everyone's attention. It worked. Everyone jumped. He learned that from Ms. Jensen. And Anna, too.

"Sit. Sit," Funny-Freddie commanded. He was clowning, but his face was pretty red. His freckles were playing connect-the-dots again. All becoming one. Freddie started talking quickly to cover up his nervousness. "Our story was 'The Emperor's New Clothes.' You remember that one," he said, bouncing his eyebrows up and down. "Well we, Randy and me, wrote a story kinda like it. Well, not exactly a story. Maybe it's a poem. But it's kinda long. And it doesn't rhyme. Only sometimes it does rhyme. Maybe, what d'ya call it? Free verse, with a little rhyme. I know, we'll give it a new name. We'll call it Free Rhyme. That's it. A new kind of poetry. A Free Rhyme story poem."

"So begin already," Hyper-Harry called. He wanted to hear the story. And he was getting tired of Funny-Freddie's long and confusing explanation.

"Okay. Okay," Freddie grinned. "This here is a Free Rhyme poem called *Stupid*." Freddie felt really good about the work they did. He wasn't wheezing because his allergies were controlled by medication. And he seemed able to read better, too. The print seemed clearer. And the words weren't dancing around so much. But he still wasn't sure of himself enough to read out loud before the class. It was easier to be the clown. Randy forgot things, but he couldn't forget to read the words with the paper right in front of him. So Freddie handed the poem to Randy. And Randy read:

Stupid

There once was a bird

Who flew to the sea.

He saw a fish and asked,

Can you fly like me?

The fish said, not I.

So the bird laughed at the fish and said,

You must be stupid.

The fish swam to the sand.
He found a clam. Where are your
Fins and tail? he asked. Can you
Swim? Don't lie. And the clam said,
Swim? I won't lie. Swim? Not I.
So the fish laughed at the clam and said,
You must be stupid.
A wave thrashed the clam
Up on the sandy shore. A dog found the
Clam and flipped it around. But the
Clam asked the dog, Can you bury yourself
In the sand? And the clam sank deep in the
Sand. The dog tried and tried to dig a hole
Deep in the sand. He buried his nose. His
Head and his shoulder, but always half of his
Hairy self stuck out. The clam
Laughed and called up through the sand,
You must be stupid.
So the dog ran to town, where he saw
A cat. He chased and passed the cat.
The dog called back to the cat, Ha! Ha! You
Can't run as fast as me,
You must be stupid.
Ha! Ha! said the cat. Try to

Follow me. Up this tree. Ha! Ha!
Laughed the cat from the tree,
You must be stupid. And on the
Branch of the tree, sat a bird.
He laughed at the cat, and said try to
Fly like me, from tree to tree.
But the cat couldn't fly so the bird said,
You must be stupid.
And the bird flew to the sea.
He saw a fish. Can you fly like me?
Oh no, not he, said the fish in the sea
You can't catch me. Stay in your tree.
And the fish swam away in the sea.
He wasn't stupid!
The End.
by Freddie and Randy.

Funny-Freddie jumped in front of Magic-Randy and talked fast. "People say if you don't know anything, or don't know how to do something, you must be stupid. But you're *not* stupid. Everyone's just good at doing different things." Freddie-the-Clown bowed. So did Randy-the-Magician. The class clapped and clapped and clapped.

"I really like your stupid poem," Ms. Jensen said. Suddenly she realized how silly that sounded. Ms. Jensen and the class laughed together. Everyone knew what she really meant.

Then the student teacher, Mr. B., walked to the front of the room. He motioned for Killer-Chuck and Silent-Amy to join him. The kids fell quiet. Slowly Amy walked up to Mr. B. She tried to stand a little behind him. To hide. Hoping he would run interference for her as she had heard him say about football. Everyone waited. They didn't even dare to look towards the back of the room. At Chuck. They waited. It was so quiet all you could hear were kids breathing.

Suddenly they heard a chair scrape along the floor. They didn't turn. They knew it was Chuck. That was how he always got up. Chuck shoved his desk aside. Yup, that was Chuck getting up. Defiantly, arms locked across his chest, Chuck clumped to the front of the room. He glared at the kids. He dared anyone to make a sound. No sounds were made. The big hand on the clock moved. Tick. Even their hearts, beating like drums, seemed to stop. To wait. Quiet.

Mr. B. moved to the side. Anna though she'd die.

There was poor little Amy, looking like she was melting between the huge shape of Mr. B. and the stone shape of Chuck. Anna knew she'd die.

Then Mr. B. began speaking. "Our story was 'The Princess and the Pea.' We decided to make it a play. I'll be the narrator." (They all knew that word because Ms. Jensen had them look it up on SR and then in a dictionary.) "Amy is the Princess." Anna noticed Amy's face wasn't red—it was purple. Anna shivered for her friend. Amy never spoke in front of the class before. Amy looked like she would pass out. But she didn't.

"And Chuck will be the Prince," Mr. B. continued.

Everyone's eyes widened. Chuck a Prince? Right! No argument. Hyper-Harry thought of saying something, but he didn't. He kept his thoughts to himself. He looked at Anna. She was keeping her mouth closed, too. That's not like her. Lucky for her she wasn't so impulsive as before. Both were in control. Quiet. The play began.

A PLAY: THE NEW PRINCESS AND THE PEA
NARRATOR (Mr. B.):

"The Princess and the Pea" is a story by

Hans Christian Andersen. Now it is a play written and acted out by Chuck and Amy.

PRINCE (Chuck): (grumbling)

Hey. I want a Princess.

NARRATOR (Mr. B.):

The people in the kingdom knew they had to do what the Prince wanted. They had to find a Princess. But it had to be a real Princess. They brought many lovely young ladies to the castle, but the Prince always said...

PRINCE (Chuck): (grumbling)

I want a REAL Princess.

NARRATOR (Mr. B.):

One night there was a terrible storm. Thunder crashed. Lightning lit up all the dark corners of the castle. It was raining cats and dogs. Suddenly a sweet voice rose through the thunder. The voice was coming from behind the front door. Everyone in the castle ran to the door to listen.

PRINCESS (Amy): (singing)

Help me. Help me. There's rain on my head.
Help me. Help me. Or I'll soon be dead.

NARRATOR (Mr. B.):

Her voice was so sweet.

PRINCE (Chuck): (ordering his servants)

Let her in!

NARRATOR (Mr. B.):

The servants pulled open the huge wooden
door.

PRINCE (Chuck): (grumbling)

Yuck! What a sight! A drowned cat.

NARRATOR (Mr. B.):

But before the Prince could close the door, the
wise Queen shouted, "Wait!" She was smart
enough not to judge the real person by her
looks. She knew this drowned cat could be the
Princess they were looking for. The Queen
drew a bath for the girl who claimed to be
a Princess and gave her a beautiful white
gown with golden threads running through
it. And after combing and drying her hair,
soft and beautiful golden-brown curls stood
high on the young woman's head. Only then
did the Queen ask her if she was a Princess.

PRINCESS (Amy): (singing)

I'm a Princess, you will see.

Test me. Test me.

A Princess I'll be.

NARRATOR (Mr. B.):

So the wise Queen decided to put her to the test. That night when she made the bed for the Princess, she put a tiny pea under twenty mattresses. In the morning she asked the Princess how she had slept.

PRINCESS (Amy): (singing)

Terrible. Terrible.

I tossed all night.

Terrible. Terrible.

It was a fright.

PRINCE (Chuck): (shouting)

Hey! A real Princess.

NARRATOR (Mr. B.):

The Prince and the Princess were married and lived happily ever after. They knew she was a real Princess because she was so very sensitive. She felt the tiny pea under twenty mattresses. And the pea can still be seen today, in a museum, in their Kingdom. The End.

Everyone stood up and cheered. Funny-Freddie

shouted, "Bravo. Bravo." Chuck never unfolded his arms. Not even when he spoke. But he was part of the play. Part of the class. No longer alone. He had actually spoken. The clapping went on and on. Ms. Jensen couldn't stop clapping, too. She was so happy. You could almost see tears in her eyes. Nope. There *were* tears in her eyes. Chuck looked away. Did he cry, too, Ms. Jensen wondered.

Ms. Jensen was proud of all the Upside-Down Kids. She didn't think they were so upside-down anymore. They were turning around. They all knew it, too. They had big smiles on their faces. But most important, the kids didn't think they were so upside down either! They were beginning to really turn all the way around. Almost *right-side up!*

Ms. Jensen went to the refrigerator and opened the freezer. She pulled out a Carvel cake in the shape of a whale. On the top, in blue icing, were the words, TO A WHALE OF A CLASS!

Everyone enjoyed the party Ms. Jensen gave. After a short while, Chuck moved quickly back to his seat. The rest of the kids ran around. They liked doing their projects, but they had been very nervous about them. And they were relieved to be finished.

Relieved that everyone liked what each other did. But they all liked their own project best. And now they were running off their nervousness and celebrating at the same time.

Chuck almost grinned to himself. He felt good. He never stood in front of the class before. But he knew he couldn't let Amy down. She was brave to sing. And he had to be there to help her. Mr. B. was great, too. He helped them. But he really let them do it all by themselves. And no one made fun. No one was mean. For the first time that day, Chuck let out a huge sigh of relief. He uncrossed his arms. Leaning forward, he put his elbows on the desk and rested his chin on his hands. Suddenly, Chuck turned his head and stared out the window. His oak leaf, that had held onto the branch all winter, was gone. But in its place, with the clear blue sky behind it, was a new *right-side-up* spring bud that had just popped open. Chuck smiled. Anna saw him wipe his eyes and blow his nose. She said nothing. But she felt it all.

11

Helping Dyslexic Children— Dr. L.'s Simple Explanation

"OKAY KIDS", Ms. Jensen began. "You've all begun to show significant improvements. And as a result, you're all accomplishing things you couldn't before. I'm sure you're all wondering if your improvements are *real* or imaginary. Whether or not they'll *last*.

"Let me first reassure you that all your improvements are real and will last. I know. Because mine did. And I can't tell you how many other dyslexics improved just like you. Many went on to college and graduate schools. Some are now scientists, doctors, lawyers, teachers, businessmen, politicians...And on and on the list goes.

"No doubt you're all wondering about Dr. L's medications. No doubt you've even considered them 'magic pills.' But they're not magic at all.

"Dr. L. already explained some of it to you in class. But I'm going to start from the beginning anyway. Just in case you didn't fully understand all of what he said. In case you forgot.

"First, we'll discuss the *medical treatment*. Then the *educational methods*. And finally, we'll explain why the various exercises work. And I'll even re-explain why colored lenses help.

"I think you kids ought to know as much about dyslexia as possible. The more you know, the better you'll feel. And the more ways you'll find getting around your problem.

"I'm sure you wanted to ask Dr. L. many more questions than you did when he came to class. That's why I'm going to be as thorough as possible in my answers—not just to the questions you asked but to the ones you thought about but were too embarrassed to ask.

"Do you know how Dr. L. first discovered that

a problem within the inner-ear was responsible for your many and varied dyslexic symptoms? Although the answer may seem simple to you all now, it was a very difficult answer to find. Most experts at the time, and even now, believed the problem was in your thinking brains—where your I.Q. is. But no one ever found anything wrong with the thinking brains of dyslexics. The only thing wrong that anyone ever found was balance and coordination symptoms—just like all you kids had and have. Many dyslexics were late talkers, crawlers, sitters and walkers. They are clumsy or klutzy. Their balance was off. Often they would fall or get dizzy and motion sick. When young, many experienced difficulties with running, skipping, hopping and climbing. Others had problems with sports such as poor hand-eye coordination for hitting, catching and batting. Others couldn't play tennis, hockey or soccer well. Lots of kids had poor eye coordination for reading or hand coordination for writing, drawing, coloring, using a pencil, tying shoe laces or cutting food with a knife and fork.

"All these balance and coordination symptoms—including dizziness and motion sickness—in very bright kids with good minds led Dr. L. to conclude that the key to the dyslexic puzzle was in the inner-ear and not the thinking brain.

"There were lots of other reasons to support Dr. L.'s belief. Because most other experts at the time thought dyslexics had a severe problem in their thinking brains, they also mistakenly thought that all dyslexics had to have severe reading, writing, spelling, math, right/left, speech, concentration/hyperactivity symptoms. And that these symptoms would always be present in severe form. But this wasn't true. The majority of dyslexics have mild symptoms. And even those with severe ones often get better—if other students, teachers, siblings and parents don't drive them crazy and make them feel stupid. These very same experts who believed this nonsense would also say that Einstein, Edison, Da Vinci, and many other famous people had dyslexia. Well, how could they have become famous if they never learned to read or write well. It's like these so-called experts were dyslexic themselves: Their minds didn't really understand what their lips were saying.

"These experts also believed that left and mixed-handed kids were more apt to become dyslexic. Dr. L. proved this wrong, too.

"They also mistakenly thought that boys were more apt to become dyslexic than girls. Once again, Dr. L. showed that boys with dyslexia are expected to succeed more than girls. So they're pressured more and they frustrate more. Therefore, they're sent to experts more often than girls. In other words, there's an equal number of boys and girls with dyslexia. Girls are just calmer than boys and so escape recognition by parents, teachers, and experts.

"In fact, Dr. L. showed that most beliefs about dyslexia were wrong.

"So finding the truth about dyslexia was not easy. It took the same determination as you kids have to eventually succeed. But all this is only the very beginning of Dr. L's research.

"Once he realized the inner-ear was related to the inability of dyslexics to read without losing their place, he invented a bunch of instruments to measure and even treat their problem. No doubt you all were given his *elephant test.*

"Do you know why he developed that test? He knew your missile-eyes were always losing their target. So he had a machine speed up the moving elephants so that they ran faster and faster. Dr. L. knew that poor missile-eyes would miss even elephants moving at slow speeds whereas good missile-eyes would target elephants moving at rapid speeds. So Dr. L. measured the speed at which your missile-eye kept missing the elephants. And that speed told him whether or not your missile-eyes and inner-ear were normal or not. If your missile-eyes and inner-ear weren't normal, then you were more apt to develop dyslexic symptoms.

"There was a very big advantage to this medical test. It could predict which kids might become dyslexic before they ever had symptoms. Do you know how dyslexia is diagnosed by others? They wait until you're very, very far behind in reading, writing, spelling, and math. Then they diagnose you. But by then it's hard to catch up once you're very far behind. Once you're feeling stupid and turned off from school. It's much, much better to catch dyslexics before they fall behind. Before they're made to feel dumb, and ugly, and fearful of reading and attending class. In other words, if you catch dyslexics very early and treat and educate them very early, you can minimize or prevent the problem from showing up.

Once Dr. L. was sure what and where the dyslexic problem was, he figured out many ways to help it. He realized that there were many medications and vitamins which ear doctors often used to help those with inner-ear symptoms like dizziness, nausea, vomiting, and motion-sickness. So Dr. L. said to himself: 'Suppose I treat dyslexics with these very same medications? If I can get these medications to strengthen or fix the inner-ear of dyslexics, maybe their reading, writing, spelling and other symptoms would improve.' And that's just what he did. And he's treated thousands of kids and adults just like you and me, and the vast majority—three out of four—get much better.

"Dr. L. also realized that these very same medications are given to the astronauts before space flights. So he wasn't surprised to learn that some of the French-Russian cosmonauts were reported to become dyslexic at zero gravity. In other words, when the medicines given them before their flights failed to work, the astronauts became dyslexic. Otherwise they didn't.

"Dr. L. even realized that he could make anyone temporarily dyslexic by spinning them around long enough. This observation also tended to prove his theory. But it gave him even more information. He knew that if you spin people around long enough and slowly enough, over time you can sometimes strengthen their inner ears. Thats why the astronauts are repeatedly given all sorts of spinning exercises before space flights.

"Dyslexic athletes often reported to Dr. Levinson that they were able to read and concentrate better when they were training for baseball or basketball or football. Other scientists noted the same thing and began recommending sports exercises and gymnastics to help kids that were learning disabled as well as those who were klutzy. It made sense that if you practiced balance and coordination exercises long enough—especially eye exercises—then things would improve. And indeed that's just what happened to many dyslexics. As Dr. L. would say it, the exercise helps their fine tuners and so the visual and hearing inputs as well as the motor outputs get better.

"I can see by your interest that all this is pretty

easy for you to understand. Once Dr. L. realized that your missile-eyes were off, he then had dyslexics read with glasses that made the letters and words bigger, thicker, and clearer. And sure enough, many dyslexic kids were able to read better with special glasses or when the print was enlarged. It was easier for their defective missile-eyes to hit big, fat targets than small ones.

"Dr. L. also realized that colored print is sometimes easier to read than black print. That's why posters have colored print—to attract the eye and hold it.

"So when researchers found that some dyslexics see more clearly when using colored glasses, it made perfect sense to Dr. L. Also, Dr. L. found that many dyslexics are light-sensitive, especially to flickering or fluorescent lights. In other words, their light-filters have holes and certain light-colors overload people. And the best way to get improvement is to wear colored glasses to filter out those colors getting through the holes. Although blue and red glasses help most dyslexics, all colors should be tested. Because you can always find exceptions.

"By the way, light sensitivity is called by its own

medical term—*photo-phobia*. And this is a symptom of an inner-ear disorder. So it was no surprise when Dr. L. found that his medications not only helped with the typical dyslexic symptoms such as reading, writing, spelling, math, and speech, but with fears and phobias too.

"After carefully studying the fears or phobias which improved on Dr. L.'s medication, it became clear that the inner-ear was responsible for these symptoms, too. This was really new and exciting. Because most people thought fears were caused by emotional difficulties—not physical difficulties like problems within the inner-ear!

"As Dr. L. previously explained to you kids, it suddenly became clear why there is a specific fear for every form of motion-sickness. Thus, for example, you can be fearful of planes, trains, buses, elevators, escalators, even walking. And, if your balance and coordination is off, you can have height, sport, and driving fears. And if your light or sound or touch filters have holes, you can easily overload and develop light-, sound-, or touch-related fears. Sometimes broken filters won't let anything in. Then you get the opposite of overloading. You can get starved for light, sound, or touch signals. And when enough signals don't come into the brain, you can get a fear of being confined to small spaces. This fear that Bob got when surrounded by my screen is called claustrophobia.

"Realizing that fears are part of dyslexia wasn't easy for Dr. L. to handle. He had been trained in school to think differently. And lots of other experts disagreed with him. But he held his ground—just like you kids have done over and over again. You've been called lazy, dumb, stupid, ugly, crazy...But here you are doing better and better. Like the steadfast tin soldier we read about in class. So to succeed, you have to be determined—whether or not you are dyslexic.

"I know what you're all probably thinking, Is Dr. L. dyslexic, too? I've thought about that myself. But I've never asked him. Could be. He's certainly determined enough. But I'll let you kids in on a little secret that only those who've read his books know. His two daughters are dyslexics. And they were fortunate enough to have their father take care of them. Between his kids having dyslexia and his seeing thousands of others like you and them, he really can almost feel dyslexic—even if he isn't.

"I know you all must be pretty tired by now. If you can still concentrate, I'll go on."

The class was quiet. No one wanted to leave. They were concentrating at peak levels. And the kids all begged Ms. Jensen to continue. They loved the stories she read them. And they liked this one best of all—because it directly concerned them. It was about dyslexia. They wanted to know more and more. They wanted to get better and better. And both Ms. Jensen and Dr. L. were really, really helping.

So Ms. Jensen continued. "Dr. L then studied the different educational methods teachers use to figure out what things work best for dyslexics. In general, he believes in not unnecessarily frustrating dyslexic kids with boring and repetitive lessons. He believes in getting your interest stimulated to maximum levels. And do you know what happens then? The body produces the same medications that Dr. L. gives to improve concentration. Isn't that amazing? He often says: 'Stimulate their interests and they won't need stimulant medications.'

"He also believes in bypassing problems and

symptoms that aren't very important. For example, he doesn't believe in driving a bright dyslexic kid crazy over his poor handwriting or spelling. I've heard him say this many times. 'Train kids to think and reason. You'll never get computers to do that. But so long as computers can print, spell and calculate, let dyslexics use them. Encourage them to go beyond these basics rather than hold up their progress until their penmanship improves or they've memorized spelling and math facts that aren't crucial. If you're bright and determined and can think and reason well, then you can always get a secretary or computer chip to do the rest.'

"It's not that Dr. L. is against learning things you have trouble with. He just believes it's often better to bypass a problem area and then come back and master it later, when you have time—if you have time. That's the way he works himself. Why bang your head against a wall when all you get is a headache? Use your mind to figure out other ways of solving or getting around problems.

"That's why I had you kids write in your books without worrying about your spelling, or writing, or grammar. I wanted you to learn to think and express yourself. That's also why we use talking books. It's important to stimulate your minds and interests without worrying about reading and recognizing every word. Eventually you'll all learn to read—and read well. And when you do, you will have listened to and 'read' hundreds and hundreds of books. The other way, you would have to wait and wait to enjoy your first book. If talking books are good enough for blind people, they're good enough for you kids.

"That's also why we use SR and calculators. It helps bypass the problem and reduce frustration. And while you're playing with these computer chips, you're learning to think and even remember in an effortless and enjoyable way.

"Dr. L. also believes that motivation is very, very important for learning. And the best motivation is that which comes from within people. People who want to learn for themselves do the best. A little fear and outside pressure are often needed. But too much is terrible. It just turns kids off. And adults, too.

"If you really, really care about kids and teaching them, they'll feel it. And eventually, they'll do well. And if you don't care, they feel that too. Then they're turned off. And, they may try to get even without even knowing it—by refusing to learn or feeling unable to learn."

Ms. Jensen was getting tired of talking. "I don't know about you kids," she said, "but I've had enough. We'll save the rest for another time."

The kids were still concentrating and glued to their seats. All Ms. Jensen could think was, amazing.

Suggested background reading
For children:
Blue, Rose. *Me & Einstein.* New York: Human Science Press, 1985.

Clarke, Louise. *Can't Read, Can't Write, Can't Talk Too Good Either.* New York: Walker, 1973.

Dwyer, Kathleen. *What Do You Mean I Have A Learning Disability.* New York: Walker, 1991.

Landau, Elaine. *Dyslexia.* New York: Franklin Watts, 1991.

Levinson, Harold. *The Upside-Down Kids.* New York: M. Evans, 1991.

For parents and professionals:
Levinson, H. *Smart But Feeling Dumb.* New York: Warner, 1984.

Levinson, H. *Phobia Free.* New York: Evans, 1986.

Levinson, H. *Total Concentration.* New York: Evans, 1990.

Levinson, H. *A Solution to the Riddle-Dyslexia.* New York: Springer-Verlag 1980.

For all—more detailed future source material:
The Upside-Down Kids-Rightside Up